It's Nothing But Pavement

Shedding the Should and Training for When the Path before You is Not Always the Path You Choose

SHANNON GRAF

Agile Artist Media

Chicago

It's Nothing but Pavement

Shedding the Should and Training for When the Path before You is not Always the Path You Choose

by Shannon Graf

eBook: 978-1-7371641-6-6

Print: 978-1-7371641-5-9

"When you recognize that failing doesn't make you a failure, you give yourself permission to try all sorts of things."

– Lauren Fleshman

Dedicated to my daughter, Layla. It is a privilege to watch you find your own way through life, as I learn to let go just enough for you to test your wings in this world.

You will always be my greatest joy, Bug!

Contents

Preface

While there are many things in this life about which we will inevitably be uncertain, one thing is certain: life hands us many curveballs, and not everything will go as we hope or plan. We can either let that keep us stuck in darker places of doubt, shame, and indecision or find ways to pick ourselves up and out of those places.

There have been many times I have sat and journaled to sort through and make sense of this life and its many moments of joy, confusion, familiarity, unfamiliarity, expectation, and unexpectedness. Mostly, I have journaled for myself, mainly when my reality and dreams have been at odds with each other over the years or when I had more questions than answers, more curveballs than clarity. Speaking of life's curveballs, one thing I never expected was to put enough structure to my thoughts and share them in the form of a nonfiction book. I'm a fiction writer, for crying out loud, I journal only for myself!

However, I had some stories worth sharing. If not for my friend, Colin Egglesfield, giving me a nudge toward sharing some of these stories and helping me believe that someone would benefit from the following words, I would likely have remained in disbelief. Telling ourselves everything we are *not* before considering who we actually are, who we could be, or who we are actively becoming is one of the many ways we buy into lies that hold us hostage in our lives.

As a reader, I desire that you take from this book the feeling of being seen and acknowledged wherever you are in your life. Whether you are just venturing out into the big unknown scary world on your own for the first time as a high school or college graduate, or perhaps you are entering the workforce for the first time in a long time, or for the first time ever. Maybe you're an empty nester, and this is a brand new chapter. It is unfamiliar. Your home has been filled with sounds, schedules, and places to be in, and suddenly, you wonder what is next.

As it is said, life is a journey. Years ago, I found an accidental hobby in something I used to view as punishment. I'm talking about running, an inevitable metaphor for life's journey. Whether training for a race or simply putting one foot in front of the other to clear your mind, having a little guidance or shared experience to lean on helps make that path before you more straightforward. Even if that path is leading you uphill or into an unknown direction with no end in sight, and you choose to navigate differently than your map's directions dictate, creating a path where there is none can be daunting and a little exciting. Either way, even my now six-year-old would agree that the journey is not linear. Children are much more inclined to venture off, following their senses with a confidence of which I find myself envious more often than not!

In sharing my experiences, uncharted paths, and ways I have navigated them, my hope is whether the path you are on is a familiar or unfamiliar one, you find what works for you: Some go-to tactics, practices, more self-awareness, and if we're sticking with this metaphor, even somewhat of a training plan. Regardless, we benefit from tangible ways to manage those moments we will all encounter. It's an honor to share with you how I've realized that the path before us, even if it's been predetermined or handed down from the expectations of previous generations, is nothing but pavement. However, how we move forward is genuinely ours to explore along the way.

CHAPTER 1

It's Never Too Late

As I was supposed to be clearing my mind while taking a running lunch break one afternoon, my mind inevitably had other plans..." I could finish the half; I've done it many times and have a solid base. Right now, I'm just enjoying running on how I feel. If I set a race goal, I must develop a training plan. Should I try for a personal best? (You may hear your running friends call this a PR). Should I try for a *big* PR? But that requires training on an elevated level. I'm just doing what I can when I can. I don't have the time (or energy!) for formal training right now." This is what I otherwise refer to as "monkey mind" chatter or intrusive thoughts. They often scampered around in my head throughout my summer of 2021 runs. I tend to encounter this "mental chatter" during my time on the pavement, despite my listening to music, podcasts or Peloton instructors along the way. Talk about a life metaphor – facing our thoughts as we journey forward! As Buddhist principles identify the "monkey mind" to be restlessness, confused, or unsettled, it wasn't much of a surprise to learn from Harvard psychologists Matthew A. Killingsworth and Daniel T. Gilbert that people generally spend 47% of their waking hours thinking about something other than what is presently taking place. They further explain that a wandering mind is usually unhappy, and philosophical traditions that teach mindfulness and presence generally lead to increased happiness. Whether a hobby, a mindfulness practice (such as meditation, yoga, or contemplative prayer), or finding a few minutes to step away from an overwhelming moment, I have found it helpful to redirect my focus, paying more attention to that which brings more awareness to myself, my thoughts, and any related feelings. What ways have you tried calming your "monkey mind" that work for you? If there is a consistent theme to those thoughts or emotions, I find it helpful to get curious about why that might be. In this case, it reminded me that I'm not done with achieving new goals, big or small, just because life has me in a different stage.

Let me take a few steps back to introduce you to the type of runner I have been. In middle school, running was dreadful. It was a punishment. The phrase, "Take a lap," was never met with, "Oh, thank God! Can't wait to get out there and run my punishment laps for leaving my gym shoes at home!" Cut to me running laps in the gym, likely wearing loafers or Teva sandals (with knee-high socks because 1990s-era middle schoolers were nothing if not trendsetters). Fast forward to high school, where my schedule gradually filled with more social, academic, and athletic activities. All these involved me being part of a group of high-energy, high-achieving peers. Don't get me wrong, I loved and thrived in these environments but was depleted of all my energy by the time they concluded. My competitive high school cheerleading squad was the group I most enjoyed participating in. Yes, I'm from Texas and was a competitive cheerleader in the nineties, so I can likely validate the stereotypes you might be conjuring up. But I digress.

After making the squad my first year in high school, I set out on solo runs in my neighborhood – for fun, for me, for something. I didn't give it much thought then, but my mind seemed to feel a little lighter afterward. My body also responded well in that the endurance training I didn't know I was doing seemed to complement my tumbling classes and rigorous schedule of competition practices. So I kept it going, and running became my own, something I did by myself, with nobody judging it, critiquing it, or stopping me to ask me to start over again. Discovering this outlet also taught me to pay attention to new and different things that resonated – it's never too late to find your "thing" or many things. It was somewhat foreign to me to find solitude at that time in my life, so it may have also been one of the first times I had to "sit" with and find some presence with my thoughts (remember, there were no cell phones to distract, and no juggling wired headphones until I would later get an mp3 player!). Running also became a go-to when I needed to work out whatever feelings I could not articulate after an argument with my boyfriend, navigating those constant high school feelings of inadequacy, or when I felt I did not have anyone to talk to. At the time, I would not have been able to tell you why I ran. Perhaps it was my way of finding mindfulness, a moving meditation to quiet the restlessness surrounding my time on the pavement. I recognized I needed to go for a run when I would experience the familiar feelings and internal "chatter" that a run would often alleviate. Eventually, the dreaded literal path of running I had been handed in my younger days eventually shifted as I found my own path and determined whether or not running would stay with me. This one still included running, though it looked different and led me in a fresh direction that would serve me in many ways.

I continued running through every chapter of my life leading up to the writing of these pages. I take it everywhere I go. It has carried me through every season of life (both literal and figurative). It has brought people into my life and enabled me to unite people. It has also helped me see parts of the world I otherwise may not have seen in my travels. Now, I hold space for it in a challenging chapter of life when finding time is a constant juggling act. However, I'm unwilling to compromise that I still need to go for my runs. These days, they often involve a stroller and sometimes a dog alongside said stroller. My hands-free days of running are fewer and further between, but it is important to me. So I make the time for it, even if it seems like it could be better or it's different from my preferred crack-of-dawn running hours of years past. Are there aspects of your life you are unwilling to compromise on, no matter what you must work around to make it work? I would say those things are pretty crucial to you, so pay attention to what value they add to your life, as they likely serve to teach you something or are a significant tool you have incorporated for a reason or two, even if you're not entirely clear on what those may be right now.

I started participating with friends in local 5k and 10k races in my early twenties. I eventually registered and trained for my first half-marathon. While the races themselves were thrilling and gave me that familiar nervous-excited feeling from cheer competition days, it was actually the training I found myself drawn to; I loved a good long run, and the half-marathon distance was a good challenge for which to train. I always had a reason to get out the door if I was going through a difficult time. If I achieved nothing else on a hard day, I would at least run, and inevitably, that would give me the momentum needed to pick my chin up enough to push through those challenging moments. I even met one of my closest friends through running when we were both new to living in Charleston, South Carolina. We eventually met up for a run, and our friendship, which has been a long-distance friendship for over a decade, was born. It was then that I realized, much like daily life, how much sweeter it can be to have some company on the run, as well.

Over time, running has been training me, but not necessarily to be an elite runner. We are all living together here on earth at this moment in time. We are all in our own race, but how much sweeter is that race when we lean on those around us who offer genuine support, company, and kindness and celebrate each other's victories along the way? The more I run, the more I see life metaphors revealed in lessons I learn on the pavement, such as putting one foot in front of the other to keep moving forward a little at a time. My finish line is always greater than a clocked time; it is my physical manifestation of mental training and makes me a better version of myself. Running gives me a safe space to practice perseverance and grace, sometimes shed some tears, and develop more strength to build upon the person and mother I learn to be daily. We all have our motivation or Why, which gets us out the door or keeps us going, especially when we would rather throw in the towel. My daughter is my Primary Why. Thankfully, all those years of leaning on my desire to get out the door and run were good practice for building life grit because motherhood is not an on-off switch; it is always on.

While my journey to motherhood may not have looked like others think it should have (e.g., dated statistics that deem pregnancies over the age of 35 as geriatric or descriptions like "older first-time mother"), it eventually resulted in my amazing daughter. It was not, in fact, too late for me to become a mother. I would not do anything differently. I don't take a single stroller run for granted because these days are precious and numbered. At the writing of this book, I recently ran my thirteenth 13.1, which was my first since becoming a mother just a little over four years ago – and it happened to be my fastest half-marathon time, even though I beat my best time by just one minute. It was a minute that represented making time for things that are a priority to me, choosing training when it was not remotely convenient to do so, logging more stroller miles than solo miles, and cherishing that my body can still do this!

More than anything that day, what meant the most to me was seeing this little girl at mile eight, running onto the course toward me, watching her mommy run toward her while doing this challenging thing to scoop her into the biggest and sweatiest hug. She was part of my training in more ways than accompanying me on those stroller miles! Seeing and being able to hug my Primary Why in the middle of a race was the extra push I needed to achieve that one-minute personal best! I will share this story with her of my one-minute personal best that happened, not early on in my much younger running days, not after following a rigid training plan, but rather on the other side of a very challenging year and four years into figuring out how to find time for the pavement while maintaining running as a single working mother. I do not intend to use this space to compare my version of challenging moments with those of others. Life can break our hearts, and we will all face challenges, moments of tragedy, adversity, uncertainty, loss, and feeling overwhelmed. These are all valid reasons to feel our various feelings and glean what we can to heal and move forward if we can do so.

It is always possible to realize a dream, and your goals are always within reach. Whether your dream is also motherhood, building a business, finding your Primary Why, or achieving a physical goal, some life moments are currently training you for what is to come and offering you tools to lean on along the way. I couldn't care less if my daughter chooses running. I hope she dreams big, practices bigger, finds her own Why, and follows through while learning helpful lessons that will serve her in life. Limited beliefs will tell us that life has passed us by; we're too old to start a new hobby, career path or explore new interests. I'm here to invite you to call BS on those beliefs, recognize when you're operating from limited ways of thinking, and practice setting out on a more intentional, empowered way forward – it's never too late to try, at least! Maybe when we realize that what lies before us is nothing more than pavement, we'll find different ways to explore our chosen directions.

CHAPTER 2

Milestones and Perceived Failures

With the door shut, as the last items were moved in, with nothing more to say, I was in my new home. Yet, it felt more like an itchy sweater that I'd never chosen to wear. It didn't fit, was uncomfortable, looked foreign to me, I didn't recognize myself in it, and worst of all, I didn't know how to escape that feeling. Looking around, it was just my black Labrador, Luther, some new furnishings purchased during the divorce to soften the blow of downsizing from our American Dream residence to a one-bedroom / one-bathroom…and me. I remember wondering, "Is this what alone sounds like?" What I could not see in those first moments, living for the first time alone, was that I had simultaneously stepped onto a new path. It would have revealed how much possibility was before me if I could see clearly. The reality is that we are not always in the right mindset to shift the focus of the lenses through which we view life when we are still emotionally on the path we left behind, whether somebody chose it for us or not.

I grew up in an environment where a fairly unquestionable life path was laid before me from as far back as I can remember. I often refer to this as a Path of Should. Many are familiar with their versions of a Path of Should. Can you think of any patterns or assumed roles from past generations in your family or culturally based on where or how you were raised? It may come with a set of expectations for how you would achieve such milestones as academic or athletic ventures, dating a certain type of person, attending certain schools, or pursuing career and family endeavors aligned with those pursued by generations before you. Some aspects of this Path determined that I should aim to be successful enough in high school to get into a good university, obtain a degree, meet and marry someone shortly after graduation, and ultimately pursue the American Dream. While these are admirable goals, they resonated less as I pursued the milestones along the way and found myself lost somewhere amongst various points of indecision. For example, having been married and newly divorced by 27 years old, I found myself veering further off of Should and at a loss for a path at all, as this had neither been modeled nor laid out as even a contingency for if and when Path of Should didn't pan out. Maybe you can identify some aspects from your version of Path of Should that eventually began to look differently than you (or someone else, on your behalf) had initially intended: Was there an expectation of you to take over a family business, live or remain in a specific geographic location, or carry out a particular way of life?

I now wonder when I began learning or accepting that this Path of Should was, conceptually, a list of expectations toward some milestone I would need to achieve along the way. Full stop. If I think back, I truthfully could not tell you that anyone in my life ever sat me down and talked me into this fictitious breadcrumb trail of milestones. So why and how did I give this path such agency over my life's direction for so long? Did I take this on by myself? Even if I had them, the answers to that question would not change the fact that we are inevitably some product of our upbringing and the surroundings we were raised in. More importantly, why would we perceive this fact as unfavorable when we can leverage it and shape our path forward? We get to make that choice now! As I move forward, I find hope that I can now recognize when I might be "shoulding on myself," as it is said. Whether or not external or internal factors initially set us out onto this Path of Should, we are likely capable of recognizing when it is genuinely someone pushing an expectation on us versus ourselves, somewhat numb to the fact that nobody is. Instead, we have formed some narrative that determines we should pursue The Thing, be The Person, or conduct ourselves in A Certain Manner. Recognizing when something does not quite sit right with you or it no longer fits is a step toward paying attention to what comes next for you.

There is nothing that levels the playing field for us like the events that come with living life: Trials, loss, illness, natural disasters, disappointments, and the moments of joy in between. This is where empathy is born if we are tuned in, but more on that later! Simply stated, life happens to all of us, and I have learned that how we adapt when those moments arise often has the potential to set us back or propel us forward. To be clear, this is not to say that the way you might choose forward motion won't come with its own emotions and opportunities to let something go. However, whether you are currently navigating your Path of Should or working towards another path altogether, we benefit from supporting that forward motion with tools that help instead of hinder us. In myself and those around me, I've seen that we often tell ourselves some narrative or story along our paths. These stories can become fact, even if they are far from it, so my challenge is to recognize what stories you might be telling yourself. Then, ask yourself how those stories are helping or hindering you.

It was surprising to learn that when heavy news or loss hits my family, I default to some variation of a fixer role before I allow the gravity of the situation to hit me. Others might default to feeling all of their feelings at the moment before drifting into another phase of the grief process. Grief is not linear, and everyone experiences it differently. In these instances, my mind poses, "What does this circumstance call for, and what can I do to address those needs?" While this comes naturally, there was a time when it came with an extra layer of what my role *should* mean. To whom, though? Nobody told me or expected me to be a fixer, just as nobody sat me down and taught me all of the "shoulds" that the role of a fixer had better assume if I was to fulfill that role.

I recognize this is a role that, for whatever reason, I go to in moments of crisis or loss. However, adding a list of expectations to The Fixer's role is less than beneficial to the mourner and those around her. The first of my four grandparents passed away in 2005. My sister and I were fortunate to grow up very close to each of our grandparents, so when my Dad's mother passed, I recall this as the first loss that hit me differently than any other. Thankfully, we had time with her. Death was and is not my area of expertise, but I did have a friend who was a chaplain at the time. I reached out to her, and she went out of her way to come and pray with the family as we surrounded my grandmother's hospital bed and provided us with guidance through what we were feeling. Each child and grandchild had the privilege of saying our final words with her, allowing her to let go when she was ready. As soon as the room was empty, my grandmother took her final breath. We knew this was coming, but nothing prepares you for the rush of mixed emotions that come and go in waves when that time occurs. I wanted to do so much to comfort us all but did not know where to begin. I recognized we, the family, needed compassionate guidance from someone like my chaplain friend. I also knew I wanted somehow to capture memories and sentiments from my fellow grandchildren and perhaps turn them into a eulogy. Writing is one of my go-to tools for working out complex thoughts or feelings, so I offered this up on behalf of the family. In the wake of a loved one's death, moments pass both quickly and slowly simultaneously. So many immediate decisions await, often while we are slogging through a fog of what just happened. A sliver of silver lining is it does not leave much room to overthink. Finding ways to fill a void or meet a need helps point you in a direction rather than getting caught in the chaos of extra expectations or missed opportunities.

"What does this circumstance call for, and what can I do to

address those needs?" is not only something I ask myself to get through to the other side of loss without a lot of percolating over what else I *should* be doing, but it also moves me to more minor actions I can take when the more significant circumstance might feel daunting and less approachable. "I'm a Fixer" is a role and corresponding narrative that helps me more than hinders me (as long as I'm working with my feelings during the fixing). Sometimes, our stories are coping mechanisms, offering a protective holding pattern. Other stories are less helpful and can become a crutch or even a lie we buy into over time.

For example, in my thirties, I reluctantly found myself in New York City's dating scene, even when I felt that I was not in a place to find and nurture a relationship. Spoiler? Those feelings are there to teach us something! Your intuition is not a fictional character. Nonetheless, my Path of Should, littered with expectations and artificial milestones, determined that because the biological clock ticks faster in your thirties than your twenties (eye-roll), I *should not* waste a Friday night on the couch when I could be meeting Mister Right, or at the very least swiping right if I was too tired to leave the couch that night. The story I bought into was something under the header of "I'm not getting any younger," "I might miss the milestone on the Path of Should if I didn't give credence to that story," and "I might miss my chance to get married again." But had I even considered *not* getting married again? Had I stopped to consider whether or not that feeling of *why* I didn't want to be dating at that time was trying to tell me something? At a minimum, I would say to Thirty-Something Shannon, "Pay attention to how you feel and then assess what it might be trying to tell and teach you." Have you ever been through a heartbreak and thought, "Here we go again; it must be me. I'm broken, too much or will never be enough."? If you are like me, that could be connected to the milestone that reminds us we surpassed some "life deadline," and the more relationships end, the further we find ourselves from the Path of Should. By the way, this is a bunch of bunk, but we are only sometimes in a place to recognize that. However, if we can learn to recognize when we find ourselves looking for some rationale to a circumstance and then discern whether that narrative is helpful or a hindrance, perhaps a rewiring can begin.

The narratives we create that hinder us are connected to the artificial milestones on the Path of Should. Personally, a crucial but clarifying question I had given little-to-no credence to on this Path was, "Says who?" I could have possibly replaced my former perception of the milestones I was supposed to reach by a given age or life stage with more intentional goals if someone, namely myself, had recognized the need to ask, "Says who?" I should go to the same university as the rest of my family. Says who? If I'm not married by 30, it is increasingly unlikely I will ever find The One. Says who? It's too late to start a new career path after 40. Says who?

I will be the first to admit that earlier in life, with each artificial milestone I missed or flubbed, came the aftermath of emotions, coping strategies, and this cloud of shame. This shame would linger in my midst as a reminder that I either did something too much or not enough to cause another bump in the road. Rather than try and learn from it, I would allow it to loom, as if I deserved to live with this cloud because of my perceived failures. I also wondered why I was unable to recognize that this path and its directions were not set by anyone else but me. At some point, I had inadvertently accepted this path, whether I felt I was too far along to reconsider or did not yet have the confidence to challenge it with another direction. While there may have been external factors that made these expectations feel unavoidable, I decided what milestones the path would consist of and where they might take place. Yet, until then, I was more a passive participant than an active one in those decisions and allowed life to happen for me, or to me, if I felt like a victim that day.

A deeper dive into psychology will reveal that much of what we operate from in our daily lives is the subconscious part of our minds. As mentioned, if we genuinely spend more time detached than *in* the present moment, it makes sense that we are more hardwired to operate from our subconscious than our conscious mindset. Our subconscious stores our past experiences, narratives, and corresponding feelings to the point that, over time, we become somewhat hardwired to operate from what our body and mind know to be true. The good news – or the *great* news – is that we can rewire, reprogram, and redirect, but it requires practice. This practice is eventually how we become more present-focused, learning to operate incrementally from a more conscious mindset. This rewiring is also known as neuroplasticity, or the brain's ability to grow and change. So how and where might one start redirecting their mindset to become more conscious and present and shift their Path of Should into a Path to Purpose? Incremental changes.

Rather than potentially being overwhelmed by the more significant life questions such as *Where do you see yourself in ten years*? Or *What do you want to do with your life*? Try starting in the nearer term. If you were to plot today's date in a year from now, then look back over the days and months the year consists of, how might you desire to recap it? What will you have filled that year with, *and how* can you reflect on it with gratitude, a sense of pride, and perhaps some progress toward your Path to Purpose?

Earlier on, I was setting myself up to live life from more of a reactive mindset instead of being proactive and specific about various avenues I could take and why. This is not to say I was wandering directionless and carelessly through life, but instead, I was motivated by my subconscious perceptions of key milestones instead of digging a bit deeper to check in with myself as to why those may or may not be for me at that time. I found myself sitting in front of my academic advisor after a rough freshman year at Texas A&M University (here's a Gig' Em, for my fellow Aggies!), trying to convince myself I needed a business degree since that's the path I had chosen with some guidance. I'd begun to contemplate changing majors. This fact alone felt like a flubbed milestone: I set out to earn a business degree and was already bailing. He asked me, "What do you enjoy, and what do you excel at?" I recall feeling relieved I could choose something under the header of 'Enjoy' regarding school and potential career. When had I relegated school and my career path to a struggle toward something that did not light me up inside? Up to that point, my moments of indecision were highly influenced by what others thought I should do, as I had yet to become adept at trusting my gut.

I was forced into a new direction by circumstances when I set out on my own at 27, post-divorce. Honestly, I do not know if I would have developed the courage to venture a new path, especially at that tender age when I already felt I was a failure because I was not ready to have kids yet. I recall taking my first solo trip to visit friends in Chicago as one of the first steps I took in a new direction: Planning a trip on my own because I wanted to, rather than for an obligation such as work or a planned occasion. It was something I chose for myself. So…was this selfish? My brain was so wired in a way that making decisions for my desires did not come naturally. I won't lie; it was a bit foreign to me to step out into this new direction without someone else to consider how I spent my time and money, but the "Why not?" mindset gradually got me over that initial hurdle. Then came a job hunt, with an offer requiring a move out of state to Charleston, South Carolina, a place I had never even visited, let alone knew anyone. However, approaching opportunities with, "Well, why not?" allowed me to take a step back and evaluate the pros and cons through a different lens. For example, why would I not take an out-of-state job and all that it entails? By and large, the reasoning came down to missing my family and friends and vice versa. To put a happier spin on it, though, I was giving them an excuse to visit what is now one of my favorite cities in the world! I decided to commit to at least two years mentally: The first to get settled, acclimated, and begin navigating friendships, and the second to make a more informed decision on whether to stay or move on. I was actively plotting a new path with purposeful milestones. Spoiler alert: I stayed past that two-year mark with absolutely zero regrets. I always encourage others to pay attention to an opportunity, *especially* when your initial reaction is a 'No' because that is likely a great time to practice asking yourself, "Why not?"

There is an important point I hope you take from this chapter, whether you have intentionally identified milestones for yourself (as I chose to practice doing for the first time in my late twenties) or you are determined to check off some milestones that were laid out by your Path of Should, for whatever the case may be. Missed milestones do not equal failure. Instead, they equate to shifting a timeline, changing your focus, or modifying the path in general. Even if your default is to perceive a missed milestone as a failure, try making the failure work in your favor so you can learn from it instead of living in it. Remember the cloud of shame? I allowed the failure to linger and was living in it. When I chose to take a small step outside of my Path of Should, albeit slightly uncomfortable, it forced me to be an active participant in one decision at a time until those small choices became more significant decisions that guided me along the path to career, personal development, relationships, and even more interstate moves. When you encounter disappointment or perceived failure, ask yourself, "What could this be teaching me?"

Perhaps you recall a gut feeling you had somewhere along the way. Guess what? Now you know how to recognize when your physical body is trying to get your attention. That is a valuable decision-making tool, so this is a win! However big or small, there is always something to take and apply. Rather than look back with pity or regret, I now try to hold space for that version of myself who just needed some time and perhaps specific life experiences to shed some light in a new direction. So hold onto what resonates, serves you, or leads you to a desire to explore (even if you don't have clarity yet), and then leave the rest on the old path. I promise you will feel lighter and closer to a step in a new, more purposeful direction.

CHAPTER 3

Lesson by Lullaby

I began writing this book two years into a global pandemic. While some days it is unfathomable that it has been this long, seeing the past couple of years through a child's growth reinforces that saying, *time is a thief.* I recall a poignant moment early on when we were first adjusting to lockdown. There was nowhere to be; I did not know how to begin processing what was becoming of our lives and simultaneously turning my home into a hybrid office-gym-child-doggy-daycare type of place. At that moment, I recognized – likely for the first time – how simplicity was there all along, holding space for us. Is this really what it took to knock me into the present moment? I recall realizing this during my daughter's bedtime routine, during which she would request two or three of our lullabies. During *Three Little Birds*, I heard the exact words I was singing to my daughter to calm and comfort her in a new way. I was singing them to myself that night. They had become words of comfort to me in that very uncertain moment. You might recognize this song best by its familiar chorus, "Don't worry about a thing, 'cause every little thing is gonna be alright." I, the adult, needed the very thing that was meant to comfort my daughter. More often than not, perhaps the comfort and guidance children look to their parents and guardians for are just as relevant to their parents and guardians. That night, a wish for my daughter became a lesson to me via our lullaby to try worrying less and somehow believe that everything will somehow be alright – sooner or later.

How often do we permit ourselves to be gentle with our needs and humanness? The more pertinent question is, when did we take on some notion that compassion is reserved for others before we recognize the need to have compassion for ourselves? I recall reading Bob Goff's words in his book, *Love Does*, and feeling his compassion permit his reader to accept the gentleness offered throughout those pages. In one chapter, Bob, a lawyer, described a technique he would advise his clients to use when they were in the courtroom. It is a physical act of letting go or surrendering by turning your palms up, particularly in times when one's surroundings would inflict the reaction of doing the exact opposite, such as clenching, tightening, resorting to closed fists, or fidgeting. Instead, he instructed the client to rest their palms on their lap, face up. I love this gesture and have since shared it with many friends, employees, family members, and even my child. Those early days of navigating the uncertainties found within the beginning of a global pandemic were ripe with the opportunity to practice a "palms up" way of life, and my daughter and I often do this at bedtime when we are releasing the day and settling into bedtime.

My Path of Should began long before I could recognize some of these needs, which I am learning to address throughout adulthood. While there have been various moments in my life that broke me down or left me feeling directionless, it was in those early moments when the gravity of a global pandemic started to hit home that I chose to check my ego at the door and surrender, palms up, to the fact that I required some comfort and guidance too. With Path to Purpose in mind this time, it was very much okay – and even critical – to acknowledge my tenderness and find ways to address it instead of numbing it. As an adult, my Path of Should would have hinted that, by now, I should have life figured out enough to pick my chin up, grind through another challenging moment, and show up for the child who needs me. What I knew to be true was that repressing my own needs had been a setback before. From a young age, I was often labeled as sensitive or even *too* sensitive – and somewhere along the way, I internalized the label of being sensitive and categorized it as another deficit of mine. My perceived shortcoming as a sensitive person led to me thinking I needed to stifle my feelings instead of learning to work with them and own them. Thankfully, I eventually gained the tools necessary to "name and claim" my feelings and, most importantly, where they stemmed from, and what triggered them. I can now accept that we are sometimes called out or labeled by others when they are grappling with their own stuff, and it has little or nothing to do with us at all. How we feel is deeply personal and valid. Fortunately, attention to mental health has become more normalized than it was during my childhood, and I now welcome a children's story or lullaby that can stop me in my tracks to remind me of an important lesson while simultaneously soothing or educating my daughter.

In those uncertain moments as a parent of a toddler, learning to navigate a global pandemic and showing kindness to myself while still maintaining some normalcy in our day-to-day lives would go hand in hand. Instead of trading one for the other, it necessitated a mindset of *both and.* The word 'and' can be empowering. I can give myself grace *and* continue caring for others. I can be overwhelmed *and* still have a hopeful outlook on life. There is even a nonprofit organization and community, of which I am proud to be a part, by the name of &Mother (founded by Olympian Alysia Montaño). Their purpose is *breaking the barriers that limit a woman's choice to pursue and thrive in both career and motherhood.* The whole reason for their existence is the "and factor" – it's in their name; they even lead with it! You may be familiar with the red light / green light connotation that comes with 'but' or 'and.' A statement followed by 'but' limits or negates anything already stated. However, 'and' builds upon the statement, contributing to it instead of taking it away. The statement, "I'm uncertain of what is going on, but I must keep going," diminishes the feeling of uncertainty. Instead, a statement that ascertains, "I'm allowed to be uncertain of what is going on *and* still strive to figure out what will be the next best decision for my family," is so much more powerful.

Can you recall moments that drummed up some need for your comfort? You could mentally return to those early weeks of the pandemic and reconnect with some of those feelings. Were you confused, wondering what information to act on? Were you scared for the well-being of your loved ones and yourself? The ability to have the awareness to acknowledge your feelings is a helpful place to start.

While many words of wisdom offer advice under a header such as, "Don't look back; that's not the direction you're going," I find it helpful to reflect and use lessons learned or input from past experiences to inform decisions on my path forward. For example, how might you navigate a job search differently today, knowing what you know now about what worked or did not work so well in a previous interview? What questions would you add to your protocol, and how might you respond to questions differently? There is a difference between dwelling on past circumstances, thus holding yourself hostage, versus utilizing past mishaps or successes to plan your next step. Taking it a step further, when you pay attention to feelings that come up when faced with a decision, sitting with it and reflecting on what that feeling is and where it might stem from can offer some hints at how to direct your decision.

As we age, we tend to recall memories from ages 10 to 30, most vividly, as adolescence and early adulthood are formative years for understanding our identity. This is referred to as the *reminiscence bump*. Additionally, reasons behind why we find ourselves on these Paths of Should in our respective lives are validated by research on the reminiscence bump. Researchers suggest that one of the reasons why we recall more events from the second and third decades of life is a set of stereotypical events that occur in a specific order, also known as a cultural life script. In a research article published in 2018 exploring the reminiscence bump, researchers Neugarten, Moore, and Lowe reported, "There are prescriptive timetables in every culture for the arrangement of significant life events (e.g., finish school, get a job, get married and have the first child)...". We are more likely to recall such events because they are linked to our cultural life scripts. But, even if we inadvertently adhere to a general life script, what about the opportunities we choose to take off-script? I have noticed two things that happen when I veer off of my Path of Should: There is some internal friction when making a choice that goes against what I previously knew, and some fear of what is to come (mainly if it was not taught or modeled for me in my upbringing). Rather than "unlearning" skills or philosophies, I more frequently learn something different or adapt previous habits along a Path to Purpose. For some, memories of childhood or years past may bring up feelings of discomfort or pain linked to trauma, and they require "unlearning" and finding ways to reset along their path. Fortunately, we are built to adapt – especially if we choose to.

Who says you need permission to offer yourself a moment to sit with overwhelm, sadness, or feelings of uncertainty? It is interesting to me when I find myself on the receiving end of a lesson I'm also trying to teach my child, such as finding calm in chaos or taking deep breaths when we are overwhelmed. What I find to be a teachable moment for her is sometimes a teachable moment for me. It would be easy for me to react and default to a bit of panic when I am trying to model a behavior I am learning simultaneously; instead, I try to practice patience with myself as I sift through tools and information to make the next decision in the direction I want to go. I use the word practice quite a bit because a reset, reframing, or rewiring of the mind (shoutout to neuroplasticity again!) requires some repetition and patience for ourselves as we learn something new over time. This may be a lonely exercise because you have to try something for yourself before you decide whether or not it will stick – and while having a sounding board can be helpful, only you can ultimately determine that. As I tell my yoga students, I am there to offer up a variety of postures and ways in which they can adapt them, but it is up to them to take what works and leave what does not. Maybe they try adding something different during another practice and find it works for them that day instead – this is what an effective practice looks like!

While I hope that our lullabies conjure up pleasant memories and feelings of comfort when my daughter hears them years later, I also hope that, in some way, I am teaching her she can also identify feelings of sadness, confusion, or uncertainty. It can be as simple as listening to a lullaby in a new way, reflecting on moments that bring comfort or conjure up familiar feelings, taking a moment to acknowledge when we feel a little off, maybe just taking a moment to sit with our palms up, or being able to say how we feel to someone we trust, inviting them into that vulnerable place as we are able. In the meantime, we never really outgrow the need for a comforting lullaby. What lullaby or moment offered comfort as a child – or even now, as a parent or adult navigating the next steps?

CHAPTER 4

Rewire Your Mind

One of my most loved movies is *When Harry Met Sally*. One of the scenes that began to resonate with me most as I morphed from a college kid, watching the movie through a very different – we'll call it somewhat naive – lens into The Real World takes place during the opening scene. Harry and Sally, new college grads, are getting to know each other as they trek from Chicago to New York City to begin their new adult lives. Harry asks Sally to tell him her life story, and she replies, "The story of my life isn't even gonna get us out of Chicago; I mean, nothing's happened to me yet!" Looking back, I might envy Sally's perspective here. She's actively driving toward a blissful unknown in pursuit of her next adventure. I, however, was focused on life through the lens of the Path of Should, for better or worse. Honestly, though, I probably had that itchy sweater feeling and desired something different. I allowed the fact that I either a) wasn't evolved enough yet to acknowledge and be alright with the lack of clarity I had about my next steps in life or b) was too scared to look at where my discomfort was coming from to move forward with more authenticity.

My recognition of when my Path of Should did not resonate *entirely* anymore and then accepting this as fact were two very different efforts. I spent most of my late twenties and early thirties pondering how to reconcile this problem rather than bringing those lessons I had learned along for the ride and leaving behind the things that no longer served me. Instead, I just threw it all in my backpack and added it to the load. When asked as a seventeen-year-old, *where do you see yourself in ten years*, High School Shannon no doubt knew that she would be married with two kids and living in the suburbs; that aligned with my cultural life script. Imagine the shame and uncertainty that instead met Shannon ten years later at 27 when she would end up divorced with no kids and in search of a next step, let alone an entirely new path. The Stoic philosopher Seneca nailed it when he said, "Every new beginning comes from some other beginning's end." (Now, you're probably humming Closing Time by Semisonic as well; for that, you are welcome!) Part of me really wanted to welcome that new beginning, one which had no clear next step, with wide-open arms. The same girl who had lived her life with a clear, albeit somewhat limited, direction of what life was supposed to look like resisted this challenge. If my yoga practice has taught me anything, it's that we often resist what we need more of, and in this case, it was a significant change.

The intersection of learning to parent while unlearning and rewiring my own mind simultaneously can be enough to paralyze me in my daily life. Thankfully, there are resources to turn to like material by Dr. Becky Kennedy, clinical psychologist and one of my favorite parent coaches. It blew my mind to learn from her that, at birth, our brains are already 25% wired for what to expect from the world and what is deemed safe. Then, by age 3, that 25% goes to 75%. Essentially, we are completely dependent on our caregivers during the years our brain is undergoing most of its wiring! Our environment so impacts us that we are then shaped by our surroundings and how life events unfold, whether colored with the practicing of faith, family traditions, stability, unpredictability, or even jarred by traumatic events. Regardless of how we perceive our past experiences, they will inevitably come alive in our present. Even if our past requires us to detangle it a bit, it can shape our present and create direction as we move forward. We get to decide what that forward motion looks like! Dr. Becky also discusses how our brain always looks to be rewired – decoupling ourselves from something that did not feel right before, and we have the freedom to change it. What might that look like for you?

Not only does life throw us the occasional curveball that stops us in our tracks and sometimes changes our direction, but there are also times when we may identify the need to change direction on our own initiative. This call for change can take on many shapes and implications. For some, it may necessitate breaking a cycle that has been ingrained in you, a cycle that may feel like it's inherent and, therefore, impossible to "unlearn." For others, failure to launch or know where and how to put the changes in motion is a roadblock that keeps them from getting stuck. This is a challenging practice, especially when unfamiliar, and the next steps call for some clarification. When we break a cycle, we try different ways of responding and learning to navigate the new life direction, relationship dynamics, ways of nourishing our body, and ways of living. This may mean leaving a situation altogether, limiting interactions with individuals, or exercising new behaviors within those environments.

I want to take a moment and acknowledge that if you, your children, or each of you are in danger, it is imperative to physically remove yourself from the environment and seek help. Please contact or have a trusted partner help you locate a local domestic violence shelter, family-oriented nonprofit, church, or local law enforcement. You will need a new path forward, which is the first step to planning to move in a new direction. The Family Violence Prevention and Services Act (FVPSA) provides funding for the 24-hour national, toll-free telephone hotline, which is available via the following:

- 1-800-700-SAFE(7233)
- 206-518-9361 (Video Phone Only for Deaf Callers)

Whether you are "unlearning" past behaviors or struggling to put changes into motion for the first time, I invite you to try a new way, something different from your typical approach to doing things. That is the mindset shift being offered here. To get started, lead with this phrase and repeat it to yourself, "Try another way." When you tend to repeat something you know has the same outcome or lean toward a familiar or comfortable way of doing something, find one way to change it up the next time. Trying something new helps me think of the intended outcome, take incremental steps in that direction, and watch how my effort impacts that outcome, for better or worse. To be clear, the goal is to make the next best decision *toward* the outcome you envision as opposed to becoming too attached to the idea of the outcome that you become overwhelmed by how you might realize the end goal.

If I become overwhelmed by the gap between where I'm starting and my hopeful goal, I freeze, and that goal sits there. I'll bring a running example back into the mix. Traditionally, I can't stand speedwork or sprinting; give me long endurance runs all day, please, and thanks! However, switching up my workouts makes me a stronger runner during those higher mileage days. My head knows this, but I must get my body to follow. A Tabata or high-intensity interval training (HIIT) approach to strength training works for me. The intervals necessitate that you put in an all-out effort for a fixed amount of seconds to earn a brief "rest" before the next interval. Rather than tell me I have to do 'X' amount of laps around a track at 'Y' speed, I am much more successful with a HIIT style workout, increasing the duration of the intervals little by little until I'm able to run up an entire hill without stopping. In other words, what felt difficult in the beginning gradually felt less so, and it positively contributed to the outcome I envisioned.

Does your commute to work take you through a neighborhood weighted with troubling memories? Find a different route or a couple of different routes to try instead. Do you want to become more active? Start by walking or jogging for five minutes – yes, just five minutes, then eight, and so on. Do you get anxious when you know you will interact with someone periodically? In advance of the interaction, give yourself 5-10 additional minutes to do something that provides you a sense of calm: Find somewhere to sit in silence, palms up, eyes closed, and listen to your breath; grab a favorite snack or song that brings up feelings of joy or calm to take you out of your head for even just a minute. You get to choose how you show up, which sets you up to lead with less anxiety. Try another way.

Venturing something new can be intimidating, which is likely what holds people back. Years ago, when I enrolled in improv classes, I had no idea just how applicable the principles and takeaways learned in long-form improv would be to everyday circumstances. After a little over seven years, I had recently moved back home to Dallas and was settling into life again in Texas. I was still traveling for work, but I wanted to find ways to re-establish some roots and new relationships in the place I called home. I realize now that, over time, my previous career dynamic of traveling up to four days out of the week for several weeks at a time was an inadvertent means for me to perpetuate my distrust in people (primarily men). Traveling solo makes it easy to blend into a crowd and even feel anonymous at times. Cut to our first class in Level One Improv when we were reminded over and over again how vital eye contact would be, not only to establish trust but to communicate to your scene partners that you were paying attention and in the scene with them. My version of trying a new way to meet people and commit to something local was a loaded and unexpected one! Day one was rooted in creating trust with complete strangers – and remember how resistant we can be to the things we need? I leaned on the "Why not?" mindset to get myself to and through that first class. As someone who has spent years observing human behavior for a living, I loved that we were all there for our unique reasons and quickly became a bonded group of adults learning a new skill, trusting each other with our quirky scene ideas, having each other's backs on stage, and walking away so enriched in our individual lives by the tools we were able to apply. Most of us even continued to the next level to build on our foundational skills. If something seems too far-fetched for where you are in life, like an aerial yoga class, rock climbing, joining that book club, or sending that introductory email to kick off a job search, ask yourself what, at your core, is holding you back. Why not give it a try?

While there are a handful of critical rules to practicing improv, its primary rule is often directly applicable to daily life. You may be familiar with the concept called "Yes, and…." There's the *and* factor again. First, 'Yes, and…' automatically makes you and your scene partner the experts at that moment, establishing a building block for that trust factor. For example, Scene Partner A might open with, "Hey Simon, since you are the reigning world champion in ballroom horse-galloping, I thought you might be able to help me out." Scene Partner B (or Simon, in this case) is automatically teed up to take and run with a name and topic if they apply the "Yes, and…" For example, "Well, yes, I am Simon, the reigning world champion of ballroom horse-galloping, and I would be glad to answer any questions you have." In the improv setting, the sky's the limit on fun, awkward, and engaging, which inevitably leads to laughs, but the "Yes, and…" approach has a similar effect in life. Rather than leading with hesitance, pessimism, or denying an idea right away, which has the potential to shut people down, you invite the idea of what could be possible as a first step. The 'yes' is affirming; it holds space for the 'and…', which invites you and others to expand upon an idea or conversation topic. It works in parenthood, too! It's a given that everyone is busy and often tired, so the desire to take additional time out with a 'Yes, and…' when you're nearing the end of the day probably sounds less appealing than just getting on with the evening routine. The next time your child asks for five more minutes, maybe you offer them a 'yes,' then your 'and' adds a little pause to engage in whatever they're doing *with* them. Try another way.

When I found myself looking for a next step at 27, that budding improviser I didn't even know existed within me said "Yes" to a job opportunity that meant taking a giant step away from my Path of Should to venture into something entirely different, new, and if I'm honest…scary. When I started thinking about the "and…" to build on the possibilities this decision could offer me, I got so motivated and energized that "No" was not on the table. I tried another way by not-so-simply leading with a "Yes," and it gradually became a new way of making decisions on my path forward. Maybe "Yes, and…" is high-intensity interval training for life!

CHAPTER 5

Does the Path Change Direction or Do We Change the Path?

"Change is inevitable, growth is optional," quoted by John C. Maxwell, is a highly relevant phrase to remember as we move through various stages of life or moments throughout the day. How we perceive the impact of change in our lives is directly related to how we experience it. Changes can be heartbreaking, complex, and even painful. And they can be more challenging when we resist them. When we get too occupied with pushing and pulling to fit life's happenings into our envisioned shape, things inevitably go sideways, and we are left exhausted and mystified as we stand in our way. How about we accept that there are ways to work with changes instead of against them?

As I have alluded to, I began taking steps aligned with my Path of Should from a young age. Scenes from slumber parties during my adolescence come to mind when, in between hairbrush microphone renditions of New Kids on the Block hits, we would play such games as the ever-trustworthy future-life prediction game MASH. This game relied on a series of inputs, informed by our small worldviews at that age, and would ultimately predict whom we would marry and whether we would live in an M(mansion), A(apartment), S(shack), or H(house). Somewhere in that midst, it was assumed we would all proceed to college after our high school graduations, certainly meet our Prince Charmings, likely live not too far from where we grew up, and raise our families in our versions of happily ever after. I realize that description is loaded with presumptions and stereotypes, and while this is a beautiful life picture, how our various milestones transpired (or did not) differed for everyone. Who is to say that my path would look differently if someone had helped me understand this more clearly from a young age?

I want to reiterate that everyone's path and how they navigate it are different - as are all of us - so why would our milestones look the same? Our paths can and will change course. I hope that something you take away from these pages reaffirms that curveballs will come your way and that you can catch them, run with them, throw them back, put them down, or dodge them from time to time. Rather than continually being caught off guard by life's curveballs, I want to shed light on ways to reframe your approach to becoming proactive on your path rather than living life in reaction to what is happening around you.

As I mentioned earlier, the milestones along the path to my career were muddled by first pursuing a major I knew was not a fit for me. How did I know? I would say had I learned to pay attention to what I now understand to be that gut feeling everyone talks about (also known as our intuition), I would have acknowledged that my lack of interest and desire to engage in my classes was not typical of me. I have always enjoyed learning and even accepting a challenge, and I suddenly had zero drive, which was amplified by the overdrive in which everyone around me seemed to operate. I needed to be more connected to who I was at my core or what I truly envisioned or desired for my future. Instead, I set out to get the degree I was told would be versatile and ripe with job offers without considering the other possibilities for which I might be better suited. So what did I cling to? That Path of Should. I was determined to get a degree in four years, be engaged around graduation, and plan that wedding, so I needed to figure out the whole degree. Thankfully, some academic advisors cared enough to help me navigate my uncertainty and find a degree program that better aligned with what I excelled at (English literature), what I thought I wanted to do (teach), and even a backup plan to support an alternate path (Psychology minor). I gradually learned what that gut feeling started to feel like – a nagging presence that something was off – and that it was up to me to figure out what that was and how to remedy that feeling was overwhelming.

I would recognize that feeling again during my student teaching semester leading up to graduation. Looking back, teaching in the classroom was my safety net versus my drive. I had been told I would be a good teacher, having been a babysitter and mother's helper since around the age of 12, not to mention I come from a long line of women who teach. Additionally, my would-be fiance was also in education, and, by extension, I was already developing a small network of fellow educators back home. The story I told myself when I was at a loss for what I would do with my degree? "I should probably be a teacher." So I ventured that path and considered being a special education inclusion teacher, a secondary education English teacher, and even considered an ESL (English as a Second Language) teaching program in Costa Rica, but I knew it felt forced. In a bit of a panic, I sought direction from my university's career center, where I received guidance that I have since offered a handful of mentees throughout my career. When I sensed my path needed a change but was seemingly too invested in changing things, I was asked, "What would you want to do if you did not teach?" I was a deer in headlights. I had no idea, as I had not considered an alternative.

The teaching profession is one I hold in such high regard, as we would be stuck without their dedication to the craft of educating us all (thank you, teachers!). Having an idea of what teaching honestly asks of those who commit to it clarified that this was not quite my gift (though I would later find my desire to teach fulfilled by teaching on the mat instead of sharing my love for yoga with others). Therefore, my advisor and I shifted focus to what summer internship options were still available for me to apply to, and little did I know that zeroing in on my psychology coursework would lend itself to a career based on human-computer interactions, which is now commonly known as the field of User Experience (UX) Research. A few takeaways from this change in course? Pay attention when you feel that something is off; for me, it feels like mental gymnastics – when I am trying to pinpoint what my mind is unsettled about and why. Look at what is going on that could be contributing to the feeling. Try another way of looking at a problem needing a decision and its possible outcomes, even if it means asking for someone else's perspective. Seeking someone's guidance led to my shift in focus away from what I thought I should pursue and zooming out a bit to an array of possibilities I could pursue. This was the first tangible "yes" in following what I now know to be my intuition or gut feeling. While your first, second, and subsequent "yes" may not always lead you to a clear path of success, the practice of trying on a "yes" before a limited thinking approach (e.g., first thinking of all the ways something could fail or is not fit because it is unfamiliar) can reveal more opportunities to consider than were on your radar previously.

If there is a consistent theme I began to see when my path presented a possible change in direction, it was the need to find some way to surrender to the process or, as we teach in yoga, find a way to sit with some discomfort when faced with a less familiar circumstance. The phrase, "What we resist persists," is reality. In my way, I fought what I was presented with because I could not see opportunity, only obstacles. In yoga, finding your breath and focusing on that function is the key to settling into a challenging posture. I had never been taught to practice slowing down, listening to my breath, and paying attention to my body's needs until I found my way to the yoga mat in 2007 – not long before my divorce. Trying to surrender to mourning the loss of marriage at 27 was not only unfamiliar, but there was no roadmap, and the process was not linear at all. I could not see straight, let alone catch my breath, to find comfort in that world of chaos. We sometimes go through the lows and eventually come out on the other side, hopefully with a new ability to find a safe place to land for when we find ourselves in this position another time. This alone can be a helpful tool when others experience something similar. For example, my best friend walked the road through divorce before me, and I will never forget what she said to me during my experience: "There is a light at the end of this. You can't see it now, but I'm here to tell you it exists." That was my comfort in the discomfort. Her words, accompanied by a beautiful bouquet of tulips, probably followed by some glasses of wine, were there to help me find my breath. I have also been able to share those words of wisdom as I walked alongside friends who have since struggled to find their way to a new path after divorce.

With the tools of recognizing a gut feeling, trying a "yes first" response, and trusting that light exists on the other side of darkness, I was presented with an option to put these into practice. Shortly after my divorce was finalized, I approached an opportunity to move halfway across the country with a different mindset than my Path of Should taught me. However, leading a decision-making process with a yes does not begin and end there, especially when it is an unfamiliar approach. I want to highlight a few ways this decision looked differently for me than it would have previously. First, when the recruiter who reached out to me introduced herself as representing a company based in Charleston, South Carolina, I listened attentively when I may have heard, "Charleston, South Carolina," and thought, "Nope! It's not Dallas, so this isn't an opportunity for me." Then I thought, "Why not at least take the first interview and learn a little more?" That interview led to an in-person site visit where, at a minimum, I would have a chance to travel to a place I'd yet to visit. Eventually, I accepted the position with an internal commitment of two years. That was my Plan A: go with the intention to stay for at least two years. Plan B (move back home if / when needed) was in my mind before I accepted because, naturally, the what-ifs and other limited ways of thinking from years past crept up. I have always been the type to strike some balance between the call to push through a challenge when tempted by the easier way out, so having a backup plan is my safety net in those Big Life Decision moments.

As life does, many more Big Life Decisions come my way, and I know plenty more are ahead of me. Change is inevitable, and having a go-to approach or tools to access when facing challenges that lead to changes certainly softens the blow. A go-to approach can also help you become more confident at making decisions as you get more familiar with your intuition and how it gets your attention, for better or worse.

A year and a half past my two-year commitment to Charleston, I accepted another opportunity to relocate again, but this time to New York City (which you may or may not know is quite unlike Charleston)! The difference this time was that it was a similar decision to one I had been presented with before, though New York City had never struck me as a livable place for someone like me. Still, I took the first interview, I traveled for the on-site interview, and before I knew it, I had two weeks to put some serious wheels in motion and make my way up the coast – even selling my car along the way, to boot! With the two-year mental commitment in my back pocket, I settled on a place in Brooklyn, a 20-minute commute from my job in SoHo, and still Plan B: If all else failed, home was waiting to welcome me back. Thus far, that gut feeling had yet to nudge me back home, though, and "yes first" continued to push me to find plenty of comfort in the sometimes uncomfortable of that concrete jungle. With two significant "yes first" decisions under my belt, I found myself more receptive to saying yes to opportunities like traveling internationally solo, accepting projects that were way out of my comfort zone, staying in New York City after a rough break-up during which I learned the importance of being okay while being alone, holding my own in the boardroom, and even leaving the comfort of the stability of a 9-5 job with benefits, (in Rockefeller Center, no less) to temporarily become uncomfortable by being my boss and freelancing for an undetermined period. Writing that last part still knocks the wind out of me a bit – who does that? Just as training for a race invites you to keep putting one foot in front of the other, in which you eventually add miles and strength to your progress, putting into practice different ways you approach life's changes can create a gradual shift in your mindset entirely.

There are many lenses through which we can look back on the

year 2020 for so many reasons and relate to each collectively, and there will always be different ways we experience it individually. The primary reason I bring this up during the chapter about change is to provide a reminder. I hope it will be helpful, no matter how near or far you are from this global pandemic, when you find your way through the words of this book. While there was so little that could have prepared me for how to persevere with life through a global pandemic, I realize now that I drew upon past life stages that had produced a little of the grit I needed in those first few months. For example, a decade ago, during my New York Era, there were several times I questioned why in the world I was living in New York City for any other reason than the job opportunities it offered. The minute you step outside and into the buzz of the city, the day has already taken off, like when you hit the 'up' button to increase speed on the treadmill a tad too much and are suddenly struggling to get your feet beneath you. You find yourself with no personal space to speak of until you reach the last step that takes you up out of the subway station into the night air as you take in a little bit more of the city before collapsing into the tiny piece of New York City that is your own space. You find yourself alone for the first time all day. The stark contrast between being part of one of the world's largest crowds, busiest work environments, and its minute-by-minute demands, and then finding yourself alone in (mostly) silence with the ringing from the day still reverberating in your head, like after a night out in college, is jarring. I now sympathize with my daughter when I have to help her wind down after an active day – decompressing is a process! That being said, learning to find calm in the craziness was and is now a daily practice.

Not surprisingly, some words of advice I received from a friend before I moved to the city were, "First you find the apartment, and then you find a good therapist; everyone needs one of each to make it here," and to this day it's one of the New Yorkiest and most accurate things I have ever heard. Thankfully, I found a good therapist who helped me realize that loneliness and being alone are distinctly different, and I would need to work through ways to find some stability in the chaos each of those stirred up inside me. There were many weekends I would want to retreat, to travel just for the heck of it, if only to escape the possibility that I would find myself in a moment of solitude. I was literally in fight-or-flight mode. Instead, I would eventually learn to challenge myself to remain in the city and aim to find time to just myself and there were some weekends when making it to Sunday night felt like the finish line of a marathon. I now realize that my introverted self being startled by the fear of solitude and slowing down may be the New Yorkiest trait I took on! Nonetheless, finding calm in the crazy, stability in being alone and lonely, and knowing that I had made it to that light on the other side of the dark (and I could do it again if needed) were the pillars I am now grateful to have built upon after practicing a few times coming into 2020.

About two months into lockdown, I learned that my partner and child's father had chosen a different path, thus leaving me to choose whether this newfound title of Single Mom would be a badge of honor or draw me back under that cloud of shame because of another perceived failure at a milestone. While still figuring out how to be a work-from-home mom and co-parent, I would then see my mother walk through one of the life stages I dread most – losing a parent. Covid pneumonia took the life of my beloved grandfather. Covid still very present going into 2021, I was then faced with the need to change jobs in the midst of my grandmother's declining health, before losing her just months before my own dad's heart attack. The Greek philosopher Heraclitus was spot-on when he said, "Change is the only constant." However, had I not tried a "yes first" approach years ago, when faced with a Big Life Decision on the other side of a devastating life change, I may not have been exposed to the breadth of ways life needed to "train me" for further changes. While the challenges that leave us with a bit of grit are not always pretty, they certainly can be grounding. If we can take nothing else out of some of the lowest lows in our lives, maybe we can remind ourselves just what we were made of that one time – so why not again? Even if "yes first" does not quite resonate, how might you try looking at a situation differently? For example, you might question why life has you amid a problem you cannot understand. In what ways may you be training right now for changes you have yet to face? I'm forever grateful that among the many great things New York City is, it offered me the playground I needed to work through my junk, training me for where I am today.

CHAPTER 6

Outcome Follows Focus

We learned several ways to cue and guide students through a yoga practice during teacher certification, and as yoga does, the practice offers ways to apply what you learn on the mat to the world around you. One cue that has stuck with me is, "Where your gaze goes, your body will follow." I often use this when students are in balance postures, reminding them to keep their chins up and find something stationary to fix their eyes on to reconnect to the breath – the ultimate roadmap in a yoga practice. This concept can be applied in many different ways. For example, in the physical exercise on the mat, if your gaze is on a moving object, you may find your pose to be a bit shaky (which creates new muscles over time – hence practice!). If you find a stationary object, you are more likely to tune into your body, focus, and find stillness. To take this concept off the mat, perhaps you struggle to find clear goals or the next steps toward your ultimate life vision. You may find it difficult to focus when many things compete for your attention daily, and life feels more wobbly than you prefer. Instead, if your mental gaze or vision is more precise, it is more likely your focus has the potential to shift to tasks and plans that align with that goal, and it eventually becomes a reality. This might sound like reasonable advice if you are adept at setting and advancing toward goals, but not everyone is wired this way. I admit that I am traditionally better at meeting smaller and shorter-term goals than "dreaming big" or setting a vision beyond the following year. Having a child changed that a bit, but I still have to be very intent, specific, and clear on what, and most importantly, how I will work towards the longer-term desires I have for my life.

Some of you reading now may be considering or starting to venture a new path, while others may generally feel you lack direction regarding what to do with your life beyond the daily hustle of making ends meet. Either way, I invite you to consider your near-term (within the next five years) to longer-term (within the next 10-20 years) objectives. If they are not yet clear, that is okay! This is a place to start. Maybe your near-term goal is to take a trip somewhere, and a longer-term goal is to purchase land you can eventually pass on to your family. Whether your goals are clear or fuzzy, consider how you spend your time outside your daily obligations. I previously mentioned how you might want to look back and recap the last year from where you are today. Where did you focus your attention, time, energy, or finances? As long as your actions are healthy and not harmful to yourself or others, these can be helpful indicators of what you truly enjoy, guiding you toward a tangible goal. In other cases, this can help you get more specific on what changes you want to implement – and why – as you move forward.

While social media offers us tiny windows into others 'worlds, which may suggest that most of us are out chasing our dreams, doing it flawlessly, with endless means to look the part, the reality is that curated life is not reality. I'll repeat it. This is not the *entire* reality of our lives we see as we scroll – instead, we see the sugary *Cliff's Notes* versions and not the cover-to-cover *Crime and Punishment* version. We are human. Life is a lot. Sometimes it is too much. *That* is reality. I want to pause and zero in on the word *outlet*, which can imply a way to channel creativity, express emotion, or physically move to generate a good endorphin high. While dreams give us purpose and daily motivations, we also need healthy ways to release our energy, retreat to activities or places that bring us back to ourselves a little, or get our bodies moving and doing something we love. Don't get me wrong, I frequently fall prey to the after-hours revenge scrolling, but as my daughter grows, I realize what a ridiculous waste of time screens can be as a means to check out. I don't need to preach about how many other unhealthy outlets exist that are even more harmful to us than excess screen time. How we treat our bodies usually indicates how we feel, as well as what we cannot say or cope with, which is why we seek outlets or settle for less-than-helpful ones. Do your ways of decompressing after a long day support or detract from your desired direction? A glass of wine with dinner can be a great way to wind down and ease the transition between the magnitude of a busy day and bedtime. However, a bottle of wine instead of dinner could indicate something is off. I would encourage someone who finds themself repeatedly defaulting to unhealthy outlets to take a look at what is going on around them, what may have propelled them to this point, and what immediate changes they can take to redirect their ways – or frankly – recognize that you may need to ask for some help. Perhaps your current outlets need an overhaul. Do you have emotional, physical, or creative outlets you can lean into regularly? If not, or you are uncertain, let's revisit some basics.

Life comes at us fast and sometimes demands a quick response or maybe even calls for determining when an aspect of life needs to change (e.g., kicking a bad habit or making a lifestyle change like getting more sleep). At a foundational level, before taking on something else, it is essential to acknowledge that we each have critical needs to meet for optimal overall health and general well-being, as outlined in Maslow's hierarchy of needs. While this may seem obvious, it is helpful to do a personal inventory occasionally to see how our most basic needs are or are not being met (and if not, identify the reasons). I call this a whole body or life scan, while others may refer to this as a form of grounding (more on that later!). Beginning with the basics, we need food, water, a safe place of shelter, clothing, and rest. Supporting those basic needs by having financial support or creating and sustaining income for yourself is foundational to meeting these needs. Beyond these basics, we need relationships and communities of support to help us realize our worth and achieve our life's work along our Paths. I encourage anyone physically or financially unable to obtain these needs to find local support via nonprofits, church food pantries, or reach out to stable family members, trusted friends, or local neighborhood groups for recommendations. When our needs are met on the most basic level, it is beneficial to have outlets to support us alongside the highs and lows of our path.

Before you put yourself into the column of all the things you are not: I am not an athlete, I am not an artist, I am not a writer, and try backing those intrusive thoughts up with stories you try to tell yourself about why you are not capable of something, lead with a yes and try something new about which you may have always been curious. For some, tapping into hobbies they have known throughout their lives becomes a natural go-to, and for others, those outlets may initially seem more of a challenge to come by if those hobbies still need to be established. In some cases, finding your outlet can also mean reconnecting with an aspect of your life that has lain dormant for one reason or another. For example, reconnecting to your faith or friendships from your childhood might lead you in a direction that feeds you spiritually or emotionally in a different way than it may have in your past. Finding a therapist and getting commentary out of your head and into the safe company of someone who can help you navigate it can also be a supportive outlet. Many fitness, sauna, and even wellness studios offer introduction discounts or package deals with no commitment, so you can try various activities or healing relaxation techniques to detach from life's demands momentarily. These will differ from person to person, so just because your best friend is obsessed with learning to crochet does not mean you will not find that you prefer a meditation app or opt for a new Masterclass course to explore instead. The key is to find activities, routines, and relationships that work for the betterment of your physical, mental, spiritual, and emotional well-being so that whichever way you venture, you can recognize when you do or do not feel safe, healthy, supported, and turn to ways to help you through those moments.

An example of how curiosity led me to try something new, eventually to a newfound enjoyment of being in my kitchen, and even a shift in lifestyle goes back to when I was still settling into my life in Charleston back in 2009, where I knew nobody upon arriving. To make new connections, I turned my focus to outlets I already knew I enjoyed, such as running – I looked up local running groups, fitness classes, or communities connected to my faith to continue exploring that aspect of my life. In the process, a coworker-turned-friend invited me to train for my first triathlon. While the sport of triathlon was admittedly outside my comfort zone, it is still in the realm of endurance training – something I loved – especially as it got me outside in my new town. Where my focus went, my new goal of completing this race followed! Our coach was practicing a vegan lifestyle at the time, and as someone who grew up in the land of brisket, I was curious. How could someone survive training for and competing in Ironman events on a plant-based diet? The researcher in me could not help myself, so I chatted with her after a training swim one evening, and she pointed me to a few books since my curiosity was piqued. Reading has always been another outlet, so I looked forward to learning something new. However, a word of caution if you want to take an inspired idea into action: it takes time and planning!

Here's a little detour to how I ventured into a plant-based lifestyle by way of failed veganism, quite the rookie mistake. While those packaged faux meat products serve a purpose, they were not meant to completely replace my main dishes at every meal or become the *only* items I ate at each meal. On days I was not fudging vegan meals with sub-par nutrition, the junk food vegetarian approach fell into a monochromatic category of carbs and cheeses. To nobody's surprise, I felt awful and sluggish, and I was doing the plant-based community a massive disservice by reducing the lifestyle to such a basic stereotype. As my goal for this new diet was unclear, starting on this path was wobbly, though new muscles in the form of awareness were developing. This is a crucial example of what can happen if you genuinely listen and learn when encountering a topic you know nothing about for the first time. Embarrassed at my lazy approach to going plant-based overnight, I learned the beauty of slowing down to move forward. I finished the recommended books to better understand various perspectives and motivations behind why someone may choose a plant-based lifestyle and the many benefits and potential drawbacks. I also began following some plant-based bloggers, got my butt into the kitchen, started exploring more plant-based nutrition, and found combinations and dishes that also supported my training. I was probably spending more time in the kitchen than I ever had. I was becoming more tuned into how being intentional with food and discovering how varieties of plants and creative dishes made my body feel, whether I was training or not. I eventually joined a CSA (community-supported agriculture), where I learned how to incorporate local crops into my meals. Let me tell you what you can do with a surplus of eggplant, tomatoes, and mustard greens! In the meantime, I was still looking for ways to expand my circle of friends. My dear aforementioned running buddy and I started a Supper Club, where each invitee was also asked to invite a friend. Before we knew it, we had a community of food and wine lovers getting together once a month, if not more. At the same time, a longer-term desire of mine was to have a family that I would eventually involve in the kitchen, share these dishes with, and help connect my would-be child to where her food comes from. While I am neither a chef nor working in the food industry, my passion for health and wellness grew when I got myself into the kitchen as a baby lacto-ovo vegetarian (meaning I still eat animal products like limited eggs and dairy) and learned the ins and outs of why I cared about my shift in dietary lifestyle so much. This is a lifestyle I enjoy to this day, the Dallas Chapter of the original Supper Club still lives on, and my daughter enjoys being part of making our meals. We even talk about having our own farm one day, but right now, we're happy with our amateur garden in the backyard.

My desire to get out into my new community via established outlets led me to a connection with someone who fostered my interest in exploring plant-based lifestyles, which led me to educate myself, experiment, and have fun with a new low-stress (to me!) outlet of cooking, use it as a means to connect with others and incorporate it into my family life. What is an area of your life where you might take a deeper look and explore an established outlet or try something new altogether? Try focusing on something that lights you up, and you might find a new direction to pursue along your path.

CHAPTER 7

Awareness, Action, and Accountability

In sharing ways I have learned to approach Big Life Decisions or even the mundane of the day-to-day, I hope you find something new to take, apply, or be reminded or inspired to revisit areas of your life that might need some TLC. While I have touched on what I learned over time to identify as my gut feeling or how my intuition personally gets my attention, it was probably not until the second or third time I experienced the physical feelings and mental gymnastics that came along with the need for me to make a decision, that I recall thinking, "I've been here before." A key pillar to creating change or adapting when change is inevitable is awareness – or being conscious instead of oblivious to what is happening around you. When we run through life on autopilot, there is less space for awareness to coexist with us; however, when we slow down and pay attention to how we feel about what is going on in our lives, we make space for more rational next steps. While it took me some time, I eventually learned to identify and acknowledge familiar feelings and circumstances, and that capability became a considerable asset and valuable tool. Recognizing something as familiar reminds us that this is not new, possibly taking us back to what kind of circumstances surrounded those feelings and, more importantly, what the outcome was or could have been, how we arrived on the other side, and what we might have done differently.

The practice of doing a whole body or life scan has been valuable in helping me identify a familiar versus unfamiliar feeling or circumstance: Am I safe? Am I lacking an essential need like food or hydration? Do I have the support I need to take the next step? More often than not, I usually experience heightened emotions as a result of a trigger or familiar circumstance that I either did not handle well or heal from previously. For example, some of the unfamiliar feelings of overwhelming uncertainty I experienced when living on my own for the first time, post-divorce, were similar to feelings of restlessness I had about five years later when I was approaching my third anniversary of living in New York City. After the fact, and with the support of a healthy outlet – therapy – I was able to look back and see the overwhelming uncertainty was tied to my inability to see a clear next step, though I knew a change needed to take place. Five years later, I recognized the feelings of being unsettled, felt that change was coming, and took a step back to assess what was happening at the moment and at that point in my life. These were familiar feelings, and I had since learned to "name and claim" (i.e., "I'm feeling restless. I know this feeling. Last time it meant I needed to make some changes to keep moving forward."); therefore, I was able to approach my path forward from a more responsive versus reactive frame of mind. Sure enough, April was approaching, which meant my lease would be up, and a decision would be required of me. My prior moves took place in April, so there was inevitably some muscle memory at play here, too, that change was coming. I was freelancing then, meaning I could work from virtually anywhere. I had been pondering another relocation primarily because paying New York City rent when I was more often living on planes and in hotels did not make much sense.

Whether you find yourself in familiar or unfamiliar circumstances or feelings, the calm that comes with pinpointing some of the reasons contributing to uneasiness is worth the years of work to get there, I promise. If you are unable to seek therapy, try having a close, trusted individual help you take a scan of your circumstances from the outside looking in. For example, I would start with some of these types of questions:

- Are you physically safe?
- Do you feel safe?
- Are you eating, sleeping, and hydrating regularly?
- How healthy do you feel? Why / why not?
- How is everything going at work?
- How are things with your family/friends/roommates?
- Has anything happened recently that caused you to feel differently?
- It's [date/month/year]; is there anything that happened around this time in the past that might bring up these feelings?

I have found that being able to help myself identify anything that might bring back some familiarity to feelings or circumstances I am experiencing can provide me with some clarity to discern what I need to do next – or not. Sometimes, I am just having an overwhelming time, which becomes a way to recognize that I am physically okay and that what I am going through is temporary. At this point, I turn to some of those outlets to accompany me along the way.

This next piece, taking action, separates two types of people: those who are aware of their needs and consciously choose to address them and those who know something needs to change but remain stuck. I get it! Sometimes, making significant sweeping changes to your life to turn things around feels like an impossible mountain to climb. However, these are choices; it is a choice to act on something and a choice to remain dormant. I feel relieved when I learn there is already a term for something I experience. "Naming and claiming" something like a feeling or emotion helps me to own it and work with it, not against it, because it feels more tangible than some thoughts living in my mind. This overwhelming feeling you may experience when faced with several decisions is also called the paradox of choice. The paradox of choice suggests that having a multitude of options can burden someone with making and then questioning their decision, as opposed to a "less is more" approach. For example, it's motivating to make grand lists of changes we intend to activate at the start of a new year to become better versions of ourselves. However, if we are not experienced in creating and activating a plan to set us up for more wins than losses, we could easily see that motivation fade by January 3rd. Anyone else?

Checking in with the basic needs in your life is essential before adding something new to your to-do list. Small, daily, and consistent patterns have the most traction when you are ready to create change. For example, if I know that I need to create more time in my day to devote intentional time to something such as – oh, hi! – writing this book, something has to give, and I need to figure out when my most focused writing time usually takes place and then protect that time. As long as I know my child is safe because she is physically with me (and writing time is usually after her bedtime or first thing in the morning), this often means putting my phone in airplane mode / do not disturb or in another room altogether. I add this small change (find the time and take away a distraction) so I am not tempted to procrastinate, and I do this each time I sit down to write so that I eventually create a habit around my writing practice. If you don't know where to start, sometimes you'll hear the phrase, "Just do *some*thing," which is not as easy to put into motion for some as it is for others, but it does have value. It is essential to start somewhere: go for a walk when you usually choose Netflix; make plans with a friend and stick to them; say yes to an invitation that you would typically find an excuse for; simply stated, change things up a little at a time.

Leveraging another wellness-focused example, let's say you have decided to take more control over your health this year and are conscious that some ways in which you have sabotaged your health goals in years past go back to some common patterns such as going out for meals instead of cooking at home, having the occasional cocktail that might turn into more than you intended, then skipping that workout the following day. Singular decisions lead us as easily toward a path of destruction as they do to paths of creation. Which do you prefer? It is not often that I crave a big, greasy breakfast if I have prioritized my workout in the morning, so I aim to move my body as soon as I can, as doing so sets me up for a better mood, better choices, and an excellent metabolism boost to start the day. If you need to learn how or where to start, think of starting small: Commit to one new habit first. I also go grocery shopping before the week kicks in and give myself a few different options so I'm not tempted to order takeout or grab something on the go when I could opt for a better choice at the ready at home. First, commit to the morning movement, then eventually add some meal prep into the routine—one at a time. My enhanced mood leads to better mental clarity at work, and a little snowball effect that starts with one habit shift becomes a lifestyle. Eventually, a weekend brunch with friends would become something I look forward to for all it entails instead of partially enjoying myself because of the shame I might feel if I've already gone out and indulged a handful of times in the days leading up to it. I can be in the moment, take in the whole experience, and not beat myself up if I want to share the sweet *and* savory option with a friend. I probably ordered the mimosa, too. Life is, in fact, too short. In his book *Atomic Habits*, James Clear refers to habit stacking in which you follow a routine behavior, such as having a morning cup of coffee, with a desired or new behavior, such as reading ten pages. Another key takeaway from *Atomic Habits* is that bad habits repeat themselves. Still, rather than come down on yourself, he encourages the reader to evaluate their systems and focus instead on implementing changes to those.

Lastly (and I will try not to stay on this soapbox for too long), I think we can all use accountability – for ourselves and to reciprocate to others. I am a firm believer that we were not meant to live our lives in isolation. Does that imply we need hundreds of surface acquaintances?

Perhaps if you're building a business, but the ups and downs in my life are highlighted with love because of the quality and *consistent* relationships I aim to nurture, I desire to keep them close for the long haul. Rather than preach the importance of quality over quantity in our relationships, I would prefer to dig into an element that creates more meaningful connections: Accountability. To be accountable to and for someone means to be a trusted enough individual to help them be responsible for their humanness:

- Decisions they need to make.
- Actions to take.
- Goals they want to accomplish.
- Unhealthy behaviors they desire to change.

What better way to show someone their value to you and your life than to bolster them with accountability? The flip side is that they would do the same for you, should you be open to receiving this aspect of a relationship. In some cases, the level of accountability a friend or family member shows me helps me determine who my most trusted relationships are and who they are not. At times, accountability may take on the form of "tough love" when a circumstance calls for you to be someone's mirror of the reality they created or perpetuated and the harm it may be causing to them or others. However, when someone in our life holds us accountable and allows us to do the same for them, it helps filter out those relationships we cannot trust and hold tight to those who stand by us, especially when life gets messy. A couple of attributes that come into play in the two-way street of accountability are the concepts of active listening and empathy. These are two crucial building blocks of a healthy relationship, whether in business or your personal life.

Have you ever been in situations where there is a conversation happening that you could be more engaged in, either because it's a topic with which you are unfamiliar or uninterested? It is far too easy to smile and nod and pretend. However, you could also try active listening and see how a few tweaks to how you listen and engage may improve your interactions: either you learn something new, get drawn deeper into a new topic, or connect with someone new by asking additional questions. To actively listen, we are invited to pay attention – another way to practice presence! Your body language will tell others whether you are engaged or not. Whether it's eye contact, leaning toward the speaker, or turning your body to face them, your posture can set you up for better listening. Rather than thinking ahead to what you want to say, listen. I will acknowledge, however, that knowing your tendencies is extremely helpful when practicing presence and being intentional. When a circumstance calls for my need to focus while participating in a social or business engagement, I know I will need to step away occasionally. I need to give myself a little space, as my introverted battery will need a recharge if I'm committed to an event for its duration. Sometimes, this helps, but other times, it's time to call it a night and get myself to bed!

We achieve empathy when we place ourselves in someone else's situation to try and better understand their position, even if we do not have the experience in common. You can use active listening to build empathy when someone is explaining a circumstance with which you are unfamiliar. You may be familiar with variations of the quote, "Be kind, for everyone you meet is fighting a hard battle" (attributed to Plato, Ian Maclaren, and Robin Williams). This quote reminds us to practice empathy, even when it is not our default response. Becoming more empathetic makes us more present in human interactions by default. In fact, and maybe I'm a product of my day job, but I often find myself taking on the observer role when I'm in a situation that calls for me to build some empathy to understand better. In other words, I'm listening to learn instead of listening to respond and simply looking at the speaker's expressions, demeanor, and body language as they tell their story, which often adds more color to it. Think back to the most recent time you may have used some active listening to develop more empathy around a situation. How did you feel?

To practice responding to a circumstance versus reacting, I have learned that I first need to get curious about what may be triggering and why – or create awareness around the situation. This gives me a foundation from which to act. Then, I can use some discernment as to when and how to put a plan into place. Lastly, having close, trusted relationships to lean on when needed is critical for giving that outside-in perspective. Over time, I've learned the value of practicing response versus reaction when met with triggers, change, and sometimes just the typical frustrations of daily life, and response is comprised of awareness, action (not reaction!), and accountability. In becoming more adept at acknowledging when you find yourself in the realm of the unfamiliar, perhaps you will begin to recognize the need to pause and consider your circumstances, whether familiar or not, more purposefully before taking the next best step.

CHAPTER 8

Get to Know Your Tendencies

Let me be clear. I did not just *poof* and figure it out one day. Where I am today is an ongoing practice, a result of becoming more self-aware over time *and* accessing tools I gravitated towards to support me. Recognizing these familiar feelings, even in unfamiliar situations, has been highly foundational to a better understanding of who I am and how I'm *inclined* to respond versus how I would *like* to respond. I'll share some supportive tools in a small variety of self-assessments. You can find free versions online, which can serve as important starting points, especially if you are doing internal-focused work for the first time. I mentioned tools I gravitated towards -- only some things stick because not everything will resonate with everyone. It depends on how receptive you are to the assessment and its outputs or implications. Some descriptions and recommendations resonate more with you and where you are right now, and they may not. Instead, they may relate to you more at a later date. Either way, I invite you to try at least one of the proposed assessment tools to understand yourself better. This is your work, nobody else's, so there is no right or wrong!

A commonly known personality assessment is the Myers-Briggs Type Indicator (MBTI), which considers a series of preferences you select and identifies you as one of 16 different personality types. I have taken the MBTI multiple times since my first time in high school psychology and consistently scored II_P (Introverted / Intuitive / Perceptive), where the only letters that have occasionally shifted were T (Thinking) and F (Feeling). While this score helped create awareness and validation of my approach or response to situations and people in the ways I always had, it also helped me navigate my needs accordingly, so I acknowledged my physical and mental cues. Over time, I have come to leverage the MBTI information and understand myself as a "social introvert," which means I can look the part of an extrovert. Still, I operate like a device whose battery will eventually deplete, even after dimming the screen, going into airplane mode, and closing out some tabs until I can recharge. The only difference is I might require more than 48 hours for a full charge! So, naturally (sarcasm), I would venture into a career path that consisted of years in consulting roles, where I would spend a week on the road with three or four days to regroup at wherever I called home before the next round. I often traveled with clients, researching various personality types in multiple cities, running through airport terminals, and schlepping all my belongings for one week because you learn to always carry on when doing multiple markets in five days. I learned the value of carrying on, whenever possible, the hard way when the Chicago Bears played in Super Bowl XLI in 2007. Rather than a stopover in Dallas for the unpack/repack routine, I tacked on a weekend trip with girlfriends to a work trip and checked a couple of bags. Since Chicago O'Hare was short-staffed due to crews calling in sick (aka watching the Super Bowl), I picked up my bag off the carousel around 5 am. This was just enough time to run to the hotel, clean up, and change into work clothes for my 8 am meeting -- on zero sleep and too much adrenaline. Just writing that gave me flashbacks, and I now have secondhand exhaustion! I would often walk through the door on returning home and decompress by needing complete silence, maybe staring at the wall, getting some much-needed sleep, and nursing myself back to a full charge over a day or two. While a couple of accompanying activities to recharge me include running, yoga, and a regular visit with my therapist, it has also been helpful to learn more about the "whys" behind my introverted-extroverted self and her inclinations.

As I progressed in my user experience (UX) research career and found myself based in New York City, I would soon identify my "subway type" as one who went face-first into a book to pass the time on my commute from Brooklyn to Manhattan. One of my first subway reads was 'Emotional Intelligence 2.0' by Travis Bradberry, Jean Greaves, and Patrick M. Lencioni. The publisher included a passcode with the book's purchase to assess and receive your overall emotional quotient (EQ) score. The scores reveal the degree to which you understand your emotions and then guide you in leveraging this understanding to manage yourself around others. This resonated with me at that point in my life, as I was studying human behaviors for a living, residing in New York, traveling globally, interacting with and living among a plethora of personalities from all walks of life, and looking for more tools not only better to understand myself but others as well. As I absorbed the book's content and assessment, I began to recognize some of the tendencies that had always been a part of me and my tendencies when interacting with others. For example, when others are upset in emotionally heightened situations, I am inclined to reach out or approach the individual(s) feeling the frustration in that moment. However, I resist that initial outreach and withdraw if I am frustrated or upset. While we all have ways of coping with our tendencies in various circumstances, the EQ assessment surfaces your recommended areas for improvement *and* management strategies, such as how to reframe your thinking and why it is helpful. Consider the strategies offered by a tool like the EQ assessment as options to see how and if they fit into your way of life, maybe now or later.

Another assessment I have yet to take since college is the CliftonStrengths (formerly Clifton StrengthsFinder), initially established by Gallup scientists. The test has 34 themes across four domains: Executing, Relationship-Building, Influencing, and Strategic Thinking. What I appreciate about this is that it focuses on elevating the positive traits of an individual. This is particularly helpful in a working or educational environment, whether you are a people manager aiming to advance your career or simply looking for another way to learn your tendencies about how you relate to the world around you. There are various payment tiers online, and the book *StrengthsFinder 2.0* by Tom Rath is one I recommend if you want to dive deeper.

Not too long afterward, I picked up Gretchen Rubin's *The Four Tendencies*, which focuses on four different ways we experience and live out internal and external expectations. It also provides readers with an assessment, tendency type, and strategies for improvement. When I received my result, which revealed my Rebel type, I was a little taken aback and humbled. One of Rebel's characteristics is resistance to external and internal expectations, which would make even more sense to me when I discovered another tool that helped me understand how my resistance might surface – and, more importantly, why.

I later learned of the Enneagram System, yet another personality typing structure with many more facets to gain an even deeper understanding of what makes you who you are and how you interact with the world around you, emphasizing the multiple facets. It may look complex, as nine personality types make up this system; however, once you learn your type and start to apply and recognize how you live it out, it becomes more simplified. I liken learning more about your personality type while using a system like the Enneagram to settling into New York City. The first time you visit? Wow. Where do you begin? How do you get from place to place without losing your sense of direction? Then, little by little, you break the bigger city down and start to learn it by neighborhoods; they become more familiar, help you feel less of a needle in a haystack, and more comfortable to the point that you begin paying attention to what makes each one enjoyable and unique versus that daunting concrete jungle as a whole.

Contrary to the perception that Enneagram is nothing more than a trend among Instagram influencers, I found my way to this assessment when I heard Suzanne Stabile as a guest on a podcast. I learned this assessment has been researched, studied, and evolved in the Western world since the early 1900s but has roots that go back even further. While there are free versions of the test you can find online, The

Enneagram Institute offers a $12 assessment online (https://tests.enneagraminstitute.com/) that takes roughly 45-60 minutes and gives extensive details on the various aspects of your type. I was intrigued to learn more about myself in this manner, so I took the leap and typed as a Nine. As it turns out, the more I learn, the more I find I am the nine-iest nine who ever did nine! The Nine are known as The Peacemakers, as they seek peace within themselves and among others. An excerpt from The Enneagram Institute's overview of the Nine:

- *They work to maintain their peace of mind just as they work to establish peace and harmony in their world. The issues encountered in the Nine are fundamental to all psychological and spiritual work—being awake versus falling asleep to our true nature, presence versus entrancement, openness versus blockage, tension versus relaxation, peace versus pain, and union versus separation.*
- *Ironically, for a type so oriented to the spiritual world, Nine is the center of the Instinctive Center and is the type that is potentially most grounded in the physical world and in their own bodies. The contradiction is resolved when we realize that Nines are either in touch with their instinctive qualities and have tremendous elemental power and personal magnetism, or they are cut off from their instinctual strengths and can be disengaged and remote, even lightweight.*
- *To compensate for being out of touch with their instinctual energies, Nines also retreat into their minds and their emotional fantasies. (This is why Nines can sometimes misidentify themselves as Fives and Sevens, "head types," or as Twos and Fours, "feeling types.")*

With another way to understand my personality and tendencies, I saw connections between my MBTI and EQ scores and my Rebel. As the Peacemaker type, it makes sense that I withdraw or lean into my introverted self to think and assess my feelings. While I have gleaned significant insight from these personality assessments, I've not crossed the finish line. Instead, these tools have served as supporting evidence for why I see, think, feel, and am inclined to respond to people and circumstances as I do. It is one thing to find significant value in realizing new or insightful aspects of oneself and another to put some of these takeaways to work!

This internal support allows me to explore and exercise ways to recognize when I encounter something or someone familiar. Whether or not you choose to dig into some of your personality types or tendencies, I hope you find ways to pay attention to what you're experiencing so that, over time, you can manage yourself and your role in the situation accordingly and, in some cases, proactively.

CHAPTER 9

Permission to Choose

In learning to practice ways to respond versus acting on feelings that stem from a reaction, I have learned some helpful principles to share with you. First, detaching your expectations from an idealized outcome is extremely helpful. Let's break this down a bit. Have you ever heard the saying, "Expectation is resentment waiting to happen."? Allow that to sit with you for a moment. During yoga teacher training, when we unpacked that which is known as the Eight Limbs of Yoga (the principles that inform and guide your purpose in life), the one that resonated with me the most was Dhyana, or the practice of being keenly aware, but without the element of judgment or attachment. For example, when traveling and through the hustle and bustle of the nuanced sounds and activity in an airport, I might be inclined to fixate on the chaos, or maybe more specifically, someone adding to the noise by talking on their speakerphone versus using headphones. If I'm attached to the notion that I prefer travel to be fluid and peaceful, I would be very disappointed and, therefore, resentful of each individual, adding to the noise or hiccups in the travel process. However, what I know to be true is that airports and travel are, in fact, a blend of unexpected changes, a bit of chaos, excessive sounds, sights, and often hilarity. Another term I was introduced to as I navigated the uncertainty of divorce was *radical acceptance*, or our ability to accept circumstances outside of our control without judging them. This concept is linked to a psychological paradigm introduced by Carl Rogers, who suggested that acceptance is the first step in creating change. Back to the airport, with practice, it is much easier to go with the flow and accept the experience because I'm less attached to an otherwise unrealistic idea of how the process *should* go.

The bonus here is that it is an even more pleasant experience when things run smoothly, and it boosts my mood during an otherwise chaotic travel day! Let's be clear, however. We would be remiss if we did not implement plans to set ourselves up to go with the flow in these scenarios. Know your tendencies: if you're prone to running late, what has worked for you to ensure you plan upfront to buy yourself additional time on the backend? Future you will thank the present you for enacting these little wins.

How about a time when you may have had expectations of someone else who likely did not know of your expectations and naturally let you down? I am guilty of this, so I'm very familiar with that misplaced resentment. A valuable lesson I learned along the way is that expecting something from others without clearly communicating and allowing dialogue will only result in the desired outcome with some tension. And the hard truth? We create so much unnecessary friction when we do this! It sounds simple: communicate. More specifically, communicate your intention, and desired outcome, work *with* others instead of harboring it in silence, and your attachment to the outcome changes. Trust me, this is also an ongoing practice because isn't that life?

Another approach to practicing non-attachment is adopting a more flexible outlook within the day-to-day minutiae of life, which does not come as quickly for some personality types who prefer a more scheduled lifestyle. Either way, preparing for the fact that life happens and things planned will require a shift from time to time can alleviate frustration when a change is needed. How does one prepare for this? Yet another cliche comes to mind, and cliches exist for a reason, right? Control the controllable. This is where getting clear on your own values and non-negotiables can support you in these inevitable life moments. In those moments, you might ask, "Is this something I can personally do something about right now?" If not, table it. This has saved me additional mental load many times when traveling, one of the multiple times I need to pivot while parenting, and generally when plans change and are out of my control.

Let's say you are the type mentioned previously who likes to adhere to a schedule of daily events. Something inevitably causes things to go sideways, thus throwing your schedule off and calling for you to reprioritize. When you are clear on what non-negotiables you have for yourself, your job, your family, etc., you might be less inclined to let a change in plans rattle you when your schedule calls for a shift here and there. Instead, you can respond by knowing which to-do tasks may have to go unaddressed or postponed that day. If you have not considered it, now is an excellent time to clarify what those non-negotiable aspects of your life are today and even in the longer term. When we have identified our non-negotiables that make up the better versions of who we are, we will find the time for them, even if it's shoe-horned into a chaotic day.

I realized taking a 'what I can when I can' mindset was something I often did with my workout routines when Bethenny Frankel mentioned this back in her talk show days. This mindset helps us to maximize the time we have available to us. For example, go for a run or a walk while listening to a work call because there is no other gap in the day to get that daily dose of time outside we all need. Listen to an audiobook instead of sitting down to read because you might be in a busy season that requires multitasking, but you are not willing to sacrifice your book club! So, instead, you listen to the audiobook after the children go to bed, and you're cleaning up around the house before winding down. This approach centers on physical activity because a non-negotiable for me is to keep my body active throughout my life. I am just not willing to give up what I know I physically need to do for myself that brings benefits to my daughter and me, both near- and long-term. Moving my body and breaking a sweat each day is one of my non-negotiables; a bonus is I can often fit in my podcasts or audiobooks while I do so – and sometimes, that enables me to finish that book for my monthly book club! Let me pause again here and be honest. This multitasking business sounds like a lot and seems on-brand in an era where maximizing our time by maxing out our energy is glorified to a degree. If I ran at this capacity all day, every day, I would not be able to sustain much else. It's crucial to my wellbeing that I know myself enough to know I am capable of 'what I can when I can' only during small windows throughout the week, often broken up between morning and early afternoon.

Another facet of my life that is incredibly important to nurture is that of the people I choose to surround myself with: your tribe, your community, your village – more buzzwords, sure – but the relationships and communities we cultivate are essential nonetheless.

Community is another non-negotiable, and my Mom Village is a pillar of my community, without which I would not be as functional daily. When we practice 'what you can when you can,' it looks something like the flurry of back-and-forth messages in the group text, where we realize there is a window during which at least a few of us and our spaces of *on-purpose* freedom sync up (when we could otherwise use this time to have lunch on our own quietly, take a Facebook break, etc.)! For example, there was a day when the children were at their respective preschools, and our realtor friend had to be physically at one of her properties while waiting for a contractor to arrive. We all knew we did not have extensive time, but rather enough time to drink coffee, catch up, and nurture this mom community with some laughs and hugs. Sure, I had to leave at the 30-minute mark to make my drive back to the home office, but that may have been the most meaningful meeting on my calendar that day. Sip coffee and catch up we did! Realtor Mom picked up a coffee carafe to-go, the moms gathered and piled in her car, and Starbucks couldn't have held a candle to our little mom-gathering. You bet we were the recharged, better versions of ourselves when we proceeded with the rest of our day.

But where does one begin identifying their non-negotiables? Personal values are a great place to start if you have not considered your non-negotiables. This might present a crossroads of sorts, mainly if you have never considered where your values stem from, whether or not they have remained true, what they mean to your life, and where you desire to go from here. As mentioned earlier, we are products of the environment in which we are raised. Therefore, as we grow more emotionally intelligent, recognize our tendencies, and tap more into our conscious mindset, we will want to revisit our values, particularly those we may have inadvertently brought along with us. So as not to reinvent the wheel, in her book *Born to Shine*, Kendra Scott offers an introspective set of questions, a synopsis of which I'd like to share here, that can guide you in exploring what you value:

- What brings you joy?
- What brings you peace?
- How do you want to be described?
- What makes you angry or upset?
- What is important to you?

- What can't you live without?
- Is there anything you avoid?

Core answers to questions like what brings me peace are unwavering. As an example, I value my faith practice. Does this mean my faith has not been shaken or challenged? Absolutely not, and even as I grow and change, my faith is steadfast. For many reasons, this is a value I hold firmly to, even when I feel weaker than I do strong. However, the physical places and people around which I practice my faith have changed over time because of how I have grown stronger in some of my values. For example, I need to be able to ask questions and discuss various aspects of the world in which we live and things that break my heart among people who share my faith-based approach to life and parenting but who may offer more varied perspectives on matters. My faith community is welcoming, without judgment or alienating others in their quest to find unity in the world where our limited understanding fails us. We lean on our faith to trust in what we can not answer or see with our own eyes. When we venture too far to one extreme or the other, we find more noise instead of simply listening. Rather, if we can meet somewhere in the middle, where dialogue is more likely, mutual growth has a fighting chance. In short, it is a non-negotiable for me to connect with others who are actively navigating similar values through the lens of our shared faith and also willing to challenge each other without contention.

Back in college, I recall a mentor asking a group of my girlfriends what our non-negotiables were for a future spouse and subsequently offered a laundry list of the things we *should* put on our lists. Once again, I was a deer in headlights. I hardly grasped my major, or – let's be honest, myself – let alone what would make up those Prince Charming-esque traits that twenty-something me would elect to desire for the rest of my life. I probably adopted someone else's version of what should be on *my* list of non-negotiables. Perhaps I could have saved myself a couple of heartbreaks along the way if I had paused first to consider how my values determined some of my non-negotiables, not only for a future partner but for all relationships as well as the general direction in which I was headed. What are some of your non-negotiables? Are these new? Have they changed – if so, why do you think that is?

The first answer to the question, *What is important to you?* is daily intentional time with my daughter. Yes, I spend most of my days with her, tending to her needs and ensuring she gets where she needs to be, but prioritizing particular time away from the daily schedule and distractions is what I'm referring to here – setting aside meaningful snippets of time. When we hold to our values and nurture our non-negotiables, prioritizing daily tasks like allocating time gets easier or more straightforward. If I want to commit to giving my child at least 10 minutes of *uninterrupted* "us" time in the morning before proceeding with our day, I will aim to make time for that each day. Consider those things you are willing to make time for in your life without compromise because they genuinely matter to you. I love how the successful entrepreneur (among many other titles) Jesse Itzler's answer to any of his four kids' requests for his time is always a yes. I would venture that someone like him places values like 'Family' or 'Fatherhood' at the top of his list, and as a result of this, allocating time to these values is a non-negotiable of his. What a healthy approach to cultivating lifelong relationships built on love and trust! Time is arguably our most precious commodity. So, how much more purposefully could we live out our days if we are clear on our values and non-negotiables and detached from an outcome that may not even be in our best interest? Getting clear on these reveals choices *you* get to make that align with what *you* deem most important. If you need it, consider this chapter your permission to make those choices!

CHAPTER 10

Purposeful Presence

Despite our best efforts, there are times when we fall into the pattern of being creatures of habit, which in turn results in the tendency to go into the 'autopilot' method of moving through various moments of the day. Maybe you can relate. If you're a parent, you are probably familiar with how your child's schedule determines the parameters of your day, especially during the school year. I know what I want to have done by 8:00 am so we can be in the car by 8:20 am because a moment later means the difference between a more relaxed commute and pushing the clock back to my desk for my 9:00 am daily work call. When about two weeks of our routine set in, I found that I didn't even have to look at the clock to know what came next. Full stop. Do we want to live life just by getting through the moments in which our lives are composed? Just getting to 5 pm... tomorrow... the next season? That's uncomfortable, and it's not how I want to model living life for my daughter. In the age of living life at a fast, faster, and fastest pace, motivated sometimes by FOMO (fear of missing out), the irony is we do end up missing out. There will always be many things we are obligated or accountable for that we do not always like, and the challenge is to allow them to coexist with things in life we desire to see and do. We inevitably need some tools and structure to ensure we check those boxes.

Again, time is arguably our most precious commodity. I realized a while ago that wishing away moments in time by 'autopiloting' my way through was just a way to numb feelings and, in turn, miss out on experiences. The word 'intention' is one that I hear folks use, but I sometimes wonder if we truly understand the depths of its implication. How do we bring intention into our day-to-day life? For many, it starts with knowing what it means to fully tune into where we are and with whom – or being intent. When I can find ways to get myself out of my head, the place where I am spinning my wheels about what lies ahead or what happened before, my shoulders release their grip on my earlobes, my jaw loosens, and I find that simplicity is holding space for me right there. One of the ways intention is defined is with the word 'purpose.' As stated, intention means doing something purposefully, which is a constant practice. Sometimes, to be present, I must allow myself to check out *on purpose.* Yet again, this is a practice, and starting small is critical when trying to implement anything into my day-to-day life. For example, if I do not make the time for 10-15 minute snippets during my workday to step away from the Desk of Screens, I am more likely to 'autopilot' than be the productive version of myself when I need to be "on" (or present!). Alternatively, I find larger blocks like a morning run or strength training session to set the stage for my day, mainly when those 10-15 minute windows are fewer and further between. I'm the type that tends to be more productive in the morning, so I invite you to find your "sweet spot" of productivity, and that could be a nice intersection for introducing a new practice in small increments.

Practicing presence or doing something on purpose might be challenging, and you must be deliberate in your boundary-setting. For example, my friends and I sometimes get to a restaurant, put our phones on a plate, and throw them at the end of the table to more or less force ourselves to be present. In this case, the boundary stems from a shared acknowledgment that our phones are a distraction and we are less present when they are within reach – especially if one tends to mindlessly check and scroll their device, rinse, and repeat *without* that word intention. I want to pause here to acknowledge that paying attention to things that take us away from our ability to be present is essential. Screens seem an obvious and relatable topic; it is hard to avoid them, which probably makes it all that more challenging to decouple ourselves from them to spend more "on purpose" time with each other, in conversation, looking each other in the eyes instead of talking into the screen (when we intend to be talking to each other). There is an ever-present tension with all of the competing noise in our lives, making it easier to tune out and default to autopilot. There is our subconscious wiring again! I'll state the obvious: life happens to us all, and the many areas of our lives that compete for our attention will always be there in some capacity.

To practice more presence, start with the notion of becoming more aware of things you do with more or less intention. It might look like acknowledging the aspects, people, or circumstances that create literal and figurative noise and feeling some pull to somehow juggle this noise with the demands of daily life. How might you generate space or limitations with a device, a relationship, or a commitment to being somewhere – but doing so with more apparent intention? You might prioritize who or what gets your time and attention over the week ahead. You might put your device in a "time out" when engaging with friends and loved ones. If you struggle with how to start practicing intention, I invite you to try the following exercise:

1. Take some time to list the things, relationships, and commitments that occupy your time or energy.

2. Identify which are part of ongoing tasks you must do (e.g., driving your child to soccer every Wednesday, being available daily from 9-5 for work).

3. Now, identify occasional commitments and nice-to-have (e.g., hosting a quarterly dinner gathering or attending a weekly fitness class).

4. Then, place them in order of importance to your overall well-

being (e.g., work might be higher because it pays your bills, and monthly book club might be a close second because social time is significant to your mental health).

5. Use the pie metaphor and allocate each listed item a percentage of the pie in terms of the value it adds to your life.

Hopefully, you now have some clarity in front of you as to what life looks like regarding how you spend your time. As a next step to practicing presence, try to identify anything that tends to compete for your attention or distract you from each of your listed items (e.g., multiple devices on your desk, those pesky apps, watching television way past your bedtime, keeping clutter in parts of your home, having your ringer on when you're likely to get higher volumes of push notifications). We can make time for the things that matter most if they are essential. Perhaps this exercise can be a tool to help us acknowledge the intersection of things that matter most, our likely distractions from them, and become more intentional with our relationships, create more focused output at work, or participate in our children's lives as the best versions of ourselves we can. If taking ten minutes to declutter each day (e.g., go through that stack of mail, throw away the dead batteries from your junk drawer) before you need to focus and this can take a little distraction off your mind, try doing this a couple of times during the week as a start.

You may still be curious or struggling to discern what gets your time and resources over things that do not. A more in-depth way of connecting yourself to what those things are or could be is to define what is purposeful for you. After all, our overall well-being is inclusive of our life's purpose, but we need to understand what that looks like, no? An exercise in discovering more about our life's purpose is found in a Japanese concept called *Ikigai* (ee-key-guy), or reason for being. In *Awakening Your Ikigai*, author and neuroscientist Ken Mogi says ikigai can also be translated as a reason to get up in the morning or wake up to joy. Who wouldn't find delight in this? To take it a step beyond oneself, the ikigai concept accounts not only for fulfillment in life but also for how this fulfillment contributes to others. So, how do we discover our ikigai? Think of the ikigai as a glorified Venn diagram of overlapping spheres, which includes:

- What you love
- What you are good at
- What the world needs
- What you can get paid for

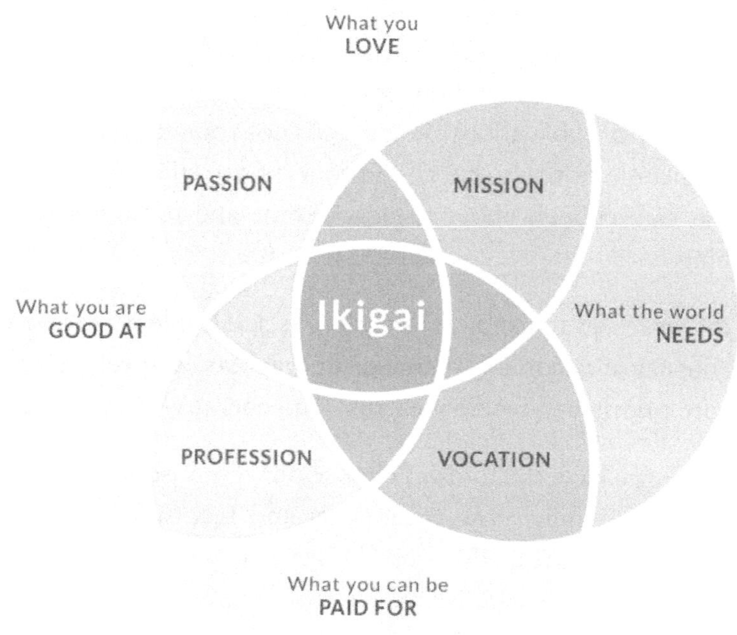

[1]

---

[1] Chris Myers, "How To Find Your Ikigai And Transform Your Outlook On Life And Business", Forbes.com, February 23, 2018, https://www.forbes.com/sites/chrismyers/2018/02/23/how-to-find-your-ikigai-and-transform-your-outlook-on-life-and-business/?sh=6a847ecb2ed4

Additionally, your passion is where what you love and what you are good at overlap; your mission is where what you love and what the world needs overlap; your vocation is where what the world needs and what you can get paid for overlap; the profession is where what you are good at and what you can get paid for overlap. The so-called sweet spot where each of these comes together is the ikigai. Let's say you are passionate about gardening, skilled at cultivating gardens and flower beds for yourself, occasionally get asked by others to advise or assist in their gardens or landscaping, and now have requests from neighbors and local businesses to assist with gardens and landscaping. According to the ikigai concept, you may have found your sweet spot.

Ideally, in discovering your purpose or that which you feel most motivated by and connected to, this exercise can give you some direction on which to base how you allocate your time and resources beyond your daily obligations. Whether or not your ikigai is intended to generate income or serve others, the concept can still help you identify what you care enough about to devote time and resources to versus something

that takes away from it. As such, it is a valuable decision-making tool. Your ikigai becomes an anchor of sorts you can reference when faced with prioritizing where your time and energy go.

When we have the tools to choose our response or what gets our attention purposefully, how we interact and feel can change for the better. All in all, we truly do control our responses; how we are or are not equipped to do so directly impacts the outcomes of those responses. Think about this! We can allow ourselves to react with our subconscious, leading to outbursts, numbness, or inaction / checking out as the norm. I am a proponent of grace and the fact that because we are human, we will sometimes be human! While this is not an excuse to overuse, give yourself a break. Do you recognize when you are numbing things out, going through motions or autopilot, reacting to something before taking a breath, or simply checking out? I would offer you an invitation to step back, maybe literally, from your desk, the room you are in, or the circumstance at hand, and practice living your life *on purpose,* leveraging active listening, leading with an empathic mindset, setting boundaries, or getting clear on your ikigai. Which of these might you try today?

CHAPTER 11

Boundaries - More Than a Buzzword

Being a realist, I understand plenty of times when choosing ways to respond versus reacting feels less viable when interacting with others. We are also responsible for ourselves, and recognizing our limitations on some issues is a skill that deserves its place in our toolbox. It is also worth noting again that these skills take practice. Taking on a new skill or using a new tool takes time, and I am steadily learning how to refine these continuously. I will add, though, that much like the old cliché of riding a bike, when you get into a rhythm of leading with empathy, listening to understand, or finding ways to practice presence, it becomes familiar and more accessible to come back to. Suddenly, it is a part of you.

Even though I skew towards my Peacemaker type, I eventually found that choosing who and what gets my time, attention, and focus at this point in my life is a much more sustainable approach to planning out my days, weeks, months – and makes it easier for me to say no at times. You might recognize this as setting a boundary – something I probably knew the definition of long before I realized I also needed to put it into practice. Much like learning to practice presence, actively listen, and lead with empathy, setting boundaries might initially feel out of reach, particularly if you lack clarity on where and how to do so. Rather than declaring to someone that you are setting a boundary, you can start by trying something I refer to as "show versus tell." Have you ever been disappointed when someone's actions do not add up to or match their words or declared intentions? Let's try the opposite, shall we?

In business and general life, it is often more practical to demonstrate or lead by example instead of explaining away and potentially risking the value of the point you want to address. In other words, choose to use your actions and behaviors over words; when you speak up, people tune in and want to listen. This might look like disengaging when you find that a conversation has derailed and may have reached the point of no return despite your best intentions. This is a default for me when I am around specific people who talk *at* rather than *with*; if there is no chance of a dialogue, I'm out. Other times, I know the other people enough to recognize our views on specific topics will likely never align – which I have radically accepted – therefore, I choose to preserve my energy and refrain from what inevitably leads to an argument. These boundaries result from having a sense of who I am engaging with, maybe even their backgrounds, beliefs, and the lenses through which they see the world. Sometimes, I can authentically remain present, listen, and observe, while other topics call for me to physically remove myself from the space and dismiss myself altogether. While some view this passive approach as a cop-out, perpetuating and even enabling someone's behavior, I counter with the fact that you have to consider the scenario. Is it work, and are you or your team and their work at stake? Are you familiar with the individuals versus more of an acquaintance with them? What is the endgame – are we convincing someone to align for a specific reason or simply finding ourselves amidst a conversation when, perhaps, a more controversial topic arises? Context counts here.

A personal example comes from the 2016 election season when I found myself in a group text that initially had good intentions of sharing information and sparking interesting conversations but eventually devolved into more one-sided aggression. I started recognizing some of my internal cues when I saw text notifications from this group. I would sigh, cringe, roll my eyes, and have a more physical response like upper body tension. When we pay attention, our body tells us so much about what we are experiencing. When we recognize these cues, we can call them familiar and draw on past experiences to inform how we might choose to proceed (or not, for that matter). When these cues became a pattern, I took back some of my mental and emotional energy by setting a boundary with a mini-strategy in mind. I would delete the thread without reading any new messages, and if the messages increased in volume, I would exit the group. As the Peacemaker type, leaving the group initially felt more contentious. Still, I intended to take back energy from that, not adding to my overall well-being, so I kept that in mind and made my peace with the choice in advance. The thread eventually grew quieter. Perhaps a separate thread persisted without those of us who chose to bow out of the conversation, which is fine. It no longer occupied any additional mental space, and I still have relationships with those people, but they rarely involve conversations around politics! This was a win-win, mainly because I set my boundaries and could keep the peace within myself and among others, which aligns with that Peacemaker inside me and feels authentic to who I am.

You can leverage the "show versus tell" approach when evaluating how to allocate your energy interactions with those around you. My Peacemaker type is repeatedly guilty of assuming people generally are not out to hurt or take advantage of others; instead -- and we have all heard the phrase -- hurt people hurt people. As mentioned, we are only partially aware of all someone is dealing with in a given moment. That said, we all recognize patterns in people who speak a lot without backing their words up with corresponding behaviors. You might recognize this type of person when you constantly receive apologies but no change in the actions that lead to the need for said apologies or when you constantly come up with a Plan B because you can no longer depend on a friend or neighbor to help you. There is a fine line between putting a wall up, becoming extremely guarded, and being a pushover. This is a prime candidate for when you can benefit from setting a boundary as a personal principle.

Over time, I have created and adopted what I refer to as personal principles. One of my fundamental principles that both limits unnecessary expenditure of time and energy and, in some cases, protects me emotionally is boundary-setting. Let's revisit the scenario of engaging in conversations that take away from instead of contributing to a productive outcome. Early in my New York City days, I attended many networking events to strengthen my business development skills on behalf of the consultancy where I worked and for my personal growth. While this was an essential aspect of my social and work life, I became increasingly aware of the draining effects these would have on me throughout the week, and some weeks, I was almost resentful of them, which is far from how I wanted to feel. These events often happen after working hours, and as we now know, I'm the type whose battery requires a recharge by this point in the evening. Armed with knowing this about myself and how my need to recharge could impede me from showing up as a more outgoing version, I would first decide if there was one event I could take off my plate that week to preserve myself for one that might be a better investment of my time and energy.

I also like to give myself a mental curfew in these types of scenarios. This way, there is a planned 'end' to this part of my evening should I feel less than my authentic self, thereby needing to call it a day. I would also ensure my physical needs were somewhat in check by grabbing a little bite to eat, either on my way or arriving and taking a quiet cab versus navigating the subway during rush hour. This is how I practiced spending what was left of my energy that day. I would then focus on what I knew versus what I needed to learn about the type of event I would be attending. For example, if it were a more significant event where I could fade into a crowd, I would have more freedom to pick and choose how and when to engage. However, in a minor event where I would be more likely to find myself with familiar faces, I would invest in those conversations early in the evening. In many cases, I also knew I would attend among a group of strong personalities who tended to dominate discussions. Rather than focus on getting a word in, I would make one-on-one connections and engage in more minor group conversations. By the time I decided to go home, was I tired? Sure. Was I satisfied with the quality I could give these engagements? Thanks to my boundary-setting, yes. I was also less resentful, having learned that knowing my tendencies helps me stay ahead of and often mitigate the onset of those feelings and emotions that arise when life's scenarios have the potential to impact my well-being negatively.

How might you recognize when your tendencies call for a personal set of principles to keep you collected, energized (or reenergized), composed, and even recovered after a draining experience? Try asking yourself and answering a set of questions such as these:

- In what scenarios do I find myself less equipped to manage emotional responses that may leave me feeling physically uneasy?
- Are there certain friends, relatives, colleagues, or even types of people that bring up feelings of anxiousness or unease?
- When I experience physical uneasiness, what helps me to feel better?

What about boundary-setting in your day-to-day life? If you're doing mental gymnastics to determine how in the world you will pick and choose what to take on and which noise to tune out purposefully, I invite you to consider starting with a look at what you want to do every day. Notice that I started with the things you *want* to do rather than those you may feel obligated to do (e.g., your job, commute, weekly commitments). However, you will likely reach a point where you need to make trade-offs. These trade-offs can change based on your needs and the demands on your time. For example, you have decided that you want your morning to include getting up early to read and enjoy your coffee before the day's schedule kicks in. Some mornings, you may find that you will choose to bypass your reading-and-coffee time, setting your alarm a little later, because you choose this trade-off for sleep to be the better version of yourself that day. Recognizing when you are spread too thin and identifying one obligation to take off your plate on any particular day can be reinvigorating. This might look like shutting down work early to finally make time to have dinner with a friend, which you know will boost your mood. Then, you get up an extra hour earlier the following day to address any leftover work needs that will set you up for a fresh and productive day. At times, the trade-off will be prioritizing our wants over our obligations in order to take better care of ourselves. While my aforementioned approach is in direct conflict with a lesson my dad stands by to this day: tackle the items you least want to do first, I find his is better suited for use in the minutiae of the to-do list I commit to within the course of my day.

In this parenting season, I often find my boundaries or trade-offs looking more like finding that one (or more) thing I can remove or allocate to another day's list (sometimes calling it a Tomorrow Problem to Fix). While I gain a sense of accomplishment on the days when my motherhood superpower to master multitasking is in full effect, the trade-off is that I'm usually taking on multiple little tasks (e.g., cleaning up the kitchen after dinner while triaging the last bit of work mail, tidying up the living room, and then going through a pile of mail) instead of heavier-lifts needed to tackle more time-consuming tasks (e.g. running errands, meal prepping, calling and scheduling appointments). I consciously take back a little energy in that moment, knowing the more significant things will get taken care of at another time. Can you step back and reevaluate your daily or weekly to-do items? What's the worst that could happen if you identify those one or two things that can wait?

If you are the type who finds it more challenging to take items off of your to-do list or end up in a state of "analysis paralysis" when trying to determine which items are most to least urgent, please take a breath!

Start with one item that week or day. Moments of indecision are rarely made easier by overthinking, panicking, or having too many voices coming at us from our sounding boards.

CHAPTER 12

Beyond the Pavement

Knowing this would be the closing chapter, I caught myself incubating and overthinking how to wrap up this talk about leveraging my meandering journey to share with you ways to think about shedding your subconscious "shoulds" while navigating the paths you choose. This is likely because, unsurprisingly, I'm still navigating this journey and its various pathways, and will be for as long as I can! This is why I continue practicing and recognizing when life invites me to take a break or train physically, mentally, and emotionally. With that said, I'd like to share some of the ways I'm currently navigating a few uncertainties, significant next steps, and pondering where to push forward versus step back, sit still, listen, wait, and find that ever-elusive comfort in some discomfort.

To assess and learn more about my overall health, I recently sought out a preventive, non-contrast MRI scan through my local Prenuvo provider. While I was pleased to see many green "good" marks on my report, they were rudely overpowered by the one in red. At the time of this concluding chapter, it has been six months since receiving test results that revealed I have an asymptomatic brain aneurysm. What? How quickly we become experts in new medical terminology overnight when news like that hits home. Allowing gravity to gradually land while keeping up with a working mom's life is no joke. The day I was to walk through the report with the practitioner over the phone, I set out for a run. I had no plan or timeframe, and suddenly, when I got a Marco Polo from that dear long-distance running friend of mine from those Charleston days years ago, I looked down to see I was almost 90 minutes into the run. She was checking in to offer words of support not long before the realtor-mom friend from Car Coffee Chat (Chapter 9) didn't ask but went out of her way to show up and sit with me during that call with the provider. Community. Palms up. Breathe.

Remember the full body scan I introduced in Chapter 7 when presented with an unfamiliar circumstance? Receiving less-than-ideal health news is currently unfamiliar territory for me. However, physical feelings — alright, total body panic — brought on by past moments of sudden news that yielded uncertainties *are* familiar. That's probably why I opted for a run right away. The feelings brought me back to what to do while planning how to navigate the next step. While taking on all of them is tempting, one step at a time is best. I reached out to my network of friends for neurosurgeon recommendations and, within a day, had a sense of direction. I got a first opinion from Prenuvo, a second opinion from my doctor, a third from a local friend's neurosurgeon husband, and validation from The Barrow Institute's Second Opinion Program (which I highly recommend). I have a plan, and we will monitor it until we need to take the next step, which would require medical intervention unless I experience symptoms in between scans. Is it always on my mind, literally and figuratively? Sure. Heh, pun intended, because without laughter, what is life? Does it get in the way of living? Not at this time, thankfully. So I choose the "why not?" approach, chase the next yes and sometimes the important no's, camp in the living room with my daughter, take the bucket list trip with my dad (we recently took his first trip to Wrigley Field!), enjoy my guilty pleasure takeout, and eliminate the noise and energy that dares to get in the way of it all.

These days, much of life happens within scheduled events, dates, or many other obligations. I find the most significant moments in the unscheduled days in between, the ones we get to choose how much or how little time we spend going and doing and dodging the FOMO instead of allowing social media to tempt us with it constantly. Incidentally, I believe Airplane Mode is as valuable a feature for us to use in everyday life as its original intent (though air traffic control and pilots might argue this point!). In those days, I also find more space to pay attention. It's no secret when we pause or slow down, our mind is left to wander, or we experience intense feelings that try to surface. We then can acknowledge our thoughts and feelings, numb them out, or save them for later. Lately, I've been incorporating more walking and biking into my weekly activities of running, yoga practice, and strength training sessions. I'm trying another way, yes. While walking and biking take a little more time, the time lends itself to being more in the moment with thoughts, listening to an audiobook, and creating more space in my day. Is it a challenge to fit it in? Of course! No day is the same, but this time to myself is one of my non-negotiables from Chapter 9. Sometimes, it is cut shorter than I'd like, but I strive to ensure it happens.

As mentioned, children are much more inclined to venture off and follow their senses, creating a path where there was once none, without judgment. We have so much to learn from children; childhood doesn't last long enough. They don't care what a map tells them; they desire to find their ways, albeit with some necessary guidance from the trusted caregivers in their lives! This begs a question for us adults when we find ourselves in moments of indecision: Are you choosing the path for you or others? I sometimes wonder how I may have navigated my path differently if I could have accessed these tools or practices in my teens or twenties. However, it's not lost on me that our lived experience can't be replaced by taking an express lane to the vital takeaway offered by someone else, based on their opinion or personal experience. Experience: A word with a meaning that toes the line between assumption and certainty, as it is only that individual, moving through a moment, an endeavor big or small, who can truly acknowledge what it feels like, looks like, and any learnings that resonate along the way. I could have speculated what living on my own in New York City might be like based on romanticized assumptions, fueled by movies or shared stories from friends, but my *lived* experience was colored with so much more breadth and depth than I was capable of ever assuming.

Would I like to go through a divorce again? Not particularly, but that redirection presented me with other opportunities I might have yet to consider otherwise. In the meantime, I grew up more and proved to myself that I could move forward. So now I pay more attention. Would I have as easily accepted the opportunity to move out of state where I knew nobody if I was accountable to this Path of Should? It was doubtful, given the limited way of thinking I had subconsciously adapted over time. I look back at both of these scenarios now. Much of what I gleaned in living on my own, physically miles away from the familiar, where it was up to me to identify the next steps on my path, would eventually apply when another role for which I could never have imagined called for the most strength I would possibly ever need to muster: Single Mother. Yet, here I am, a few years in. How? Well, myriad reasons have led me to where I am. However, when presented with the option to resist or persist, finding the tools to persevere has served me best, though it certainly took a lot of work in the near term. Training. These twists and turns on my path were similar to how often I have spent miles on the pavement preparing for the next big race. Along the way, you find which shoes and attire work best, whether or not to carry a handheld bottle or wing it, and trust there will be enough stocked water stations. You figure out which fuel works best before, during, and post-run, who to take advice from, and possibly open yourself up to train with others as the miles stack up and the finish line feels further and further from something attainable. As long as you put in the work and actually train, someone along the way inevitably reminds you as you approach race day to "Trust your training!" Even on race day, though, no matter how hydrated, fueled, prepared, and rested (wait – is anyone really rested on race day?) we might be, we do not control things like the weather, how our body may respond, or many uncontrollable factors that can impact our day to day. However, a rocky start does not have to set the tone for the road ahead or how strong we finish.

As you know, I have navigated a few seasons of training for life beyond the pavement. However, the pavement has been an excellent teacher and constant companion for which I'm grateful. However, it's just pavement. I build strength during the in-between moments. The moments where the training happens on and around the path and lead to the next event truly matter.

Where and how is life possibly training you at this time? Who is walking alongside you? How well-equipped do you feel to trust yourself? Do you know your tendencies in both familiar or unfamiliar circumstances or surroundings? Regardless of your path or the directions you have taken, each step becomes part of you. Your experience matters, so why not consider what it teaches you in this training season?

I ultimately decided (with a few friendly nudges) to share with you some of my "training tips" that have supported my decisions along the way primarily because, much like the road to race day, we are unable to determine our outcomes, but we sure can move forward – and finding what that forward movement will consist of might lend us enough of that "finish line feeling" to motivate our way to the following starting line. Look around, and you might find you are already on your mark, getting set, just waiting for someone to say go! Well, here you are then: Go!

Acknowledgements

I am extremely grateful to everyone who contributed to the realization of this book. Telling my story through these pages has been a journey, and I am fortunate to have had the ongoing support and encouragement of so many people in my life along the way. At one point, I almost decided to keep this book to myself only to share with those close to me one day. With thanks to the following folks, I ultimately chose to finish this book and make it publicly available.

First and foremost, thank you to my family, my cheerleaders from day one. You have always stood by me and supported my dreams. Mom, Dad, and Kacie, your unwavering support and presence in my life keep me going each day – you have always been dependable and encouraging, and I am happy to share this accomplishment with you.

To Colin, who encouraged me from the inception of this idea to tell my own story instead of the fiction stories I initially pitched you. While those may happen someday, it was your steadfast confidence in me to trust myself and that, even if only one person takes something to apply to their path, this book has a purpose. Thank you for providing the platform and resources to realize this dream of mine!

My sincere thanks to my editor, Tracy, whose patience, feedback, and guidance contributed significantly to the quality of this manuscript. Your commitment to the success of this project is truly commendable and your gentle reminders that, "People need this book," are to thank for its completion.

To Cheyenne, thank you for bringing my cover art vision to life and being my social media guru with your many talents; it's a privilege to know you and work alongside you.

A special thanks to the friends and beta readers who celebrated many milestones along the way with me, as I embarked upon and completed this endeavor. Thank you for asking me how it was going, and encouraging me to talk about it – you helped me to keep the goal ever present on the days I found it challenging to show up and write.

To my precious girl, Layla Emerson, my Why. Ultimately, you are the reason I finished this book. I wanted you to have this training guide at any point in time you needed some guidance to lean on, as a reminder to keep dreaming, seeking, and living your own story. Though I am never too far away to be there for you, may these words also give you hope and inspiration to persevere and find your way.

I would also like to acknowledge my teachers and countless authors whose work and instruction have inspired and informed my writing. You never know when your inspiration will light a fire in someone.

Lastly, I want to thank the readers. Your interest and engagement make this process worthwhile and I sincerely hope you find something about yourself to put into action, share with others, or simply ponder as you find your next steps along your path!